JUSTIN JACKSON

Marketing for Developers

Build, launch, and get your first 100 customers

First edition

This book was professionally typeset on Reedsy.
Find out more at reedsy.com

Contents

Hello world

In 1983 my family got a Commodore VIC-20. One of the first things I did was create a "Hello World" application in BASIC. Ever since then, I've wanted to make stuff with computers.

From an early age, I loved that technology enabled individuals to create something and share it with the world. When I was eleven, I sent Apogee Software a $44 check in the mail for a game called Commander Keen. The order form looked like this:

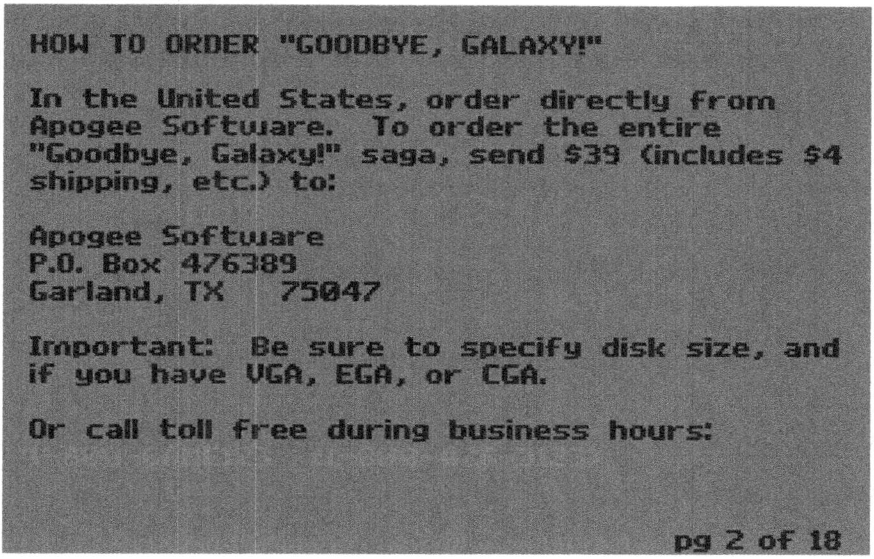

HOW TO ORDER "GOODBYE, GALAXY!"

In the United States, order directly from Apogee Software. To order the entire "Goodbye, Galaxy!" saga, send $39 (includes $4 shipping, etc.) to:

Apogee Software
P.O. Box 476389
Garland, TX 75047

Important: Be sure to specify disk size, and if you have VGA, EGA, or CGA.

Or call toll free during business hours:

pg 2 of 18

These indie developers in Texas distributed this shareware game on Usenet groups and bulletin boards. Crazy enough, kids like me found them and bought them!

What is marketing? It's the ability to get our product into the hands of customers. Before modems, bulletin boards and the Internet, this was difficult. The problem was distribution: you could only buy software in retail stores.

Today, distribution is democratized. There are still gatekeepers, like Apple and their App Store, but there are fewer barriers to entry. There's no better time than now to be a software developer, and now is a great time to build and launch your product.

Who should read this book?

This book is for developers who want to earn an income from the products they create. I wrote it specifically for these three stages:

1. Developers who want to build a product, but haven't found an idea.
2. Developers who are building a product, but haven't yet launched.
3. Developers who have launched, and are looking for their first 100 customers.

These tactics will also be useful for startups and teams to review together.

My friend Patrick Mckenzie has this great quote:

> *"As developers, you can create things, which is magical."*

You can build the application; this book will help you to launch it to paying customers.

Is marketing necessary?

We've all heard stories about developers who built something and had it magically succeed.

One example is the story of a 29-year-old developer named Dong Nguyen. In May 2013, from his home in Vietnam, he quietly released a mobile game called Flappy Bird. It existed in obscurity for six months, registering only a handful of downloads.

Suddenly, on February 1, the game's popularity exploded. Flappy Bird was discovered and downloaded by millions of people. It climbed to the top of the iTunes and Google Play charts. Nguyen was earning more than $50,000 a day in advertising royalties.

He claimed multiple times that he hadn't paid to boost the game's rankings. If he became a success without marketing, why can't we?

Unicorns and outliers

First, we have to admit that Nguyen's success is unusual. Scan the top-charting apps, and you'll see names like Facebook, Instagram, Snapchat, YouTube, Netflix, and Pandora. These are companies with serious marketing muscle.

An indie app can climb the charts to number 1, but it's not common. It's even harder to make a profit. The analyst firm Gartner found that:

> *Less than 0.01 percent of consumer mobile apps will be considered a financial success by their developers.*[1]

My goal is to help you beat these odds. I want you to earn revenue from the software you create. It's possible, but we're not going to get there by following unicorns. Instead, we need to follow principles that are tested and are replicable.

Survivor bias

Our tendency as humans to only focus on successful examples (while ignoring the hundreds, or thousands of failures) is called *survivorship bias*.

---

[1] www.gartner.com/newsroom/id/2648515

> *"The behaviors of winners are remembered and dissected far more thoroughly than those of losers, and given greater weight."*
> *- Freakonomics*[2]

How many other developers submitted apps, and did not achieve Dong Nguyen's success? Likely thousands.

In fact, a French developer had published a very similar game to the Google Play store in 2011, called Piou Piou. The gameplay, graphics, and mechanics are almost identical, and yet it did not meet Flappy Bird's fame.

Flappy Bird (2013) vs. Piou Piou (2011)

Not all success stories are helpful. Dong Nguyen himself doesn't know why Flappy Bird became a hit. What did he do right and the thousands of other developers do wrong? We don't know, and therefore can't extrapolate a winning formula from his experience.

> *"If you group successes together and look for what makes them similar, the only real answer will be luck."*

---

2 freakonomics.com/2009/09/17/survivor-bias-on-the-gridiron/

- Daniel Kahneman, Thinking Fast and Slow

You can increase your odds

If it's all about luck, then why bother?

You can increase your odds of success. Founders who discover what people want, and build a solid product to meet that need, have a huge advantage. After that, marketing skills will give your product a better chance of being discovered.

Let's go back to Flappy Bird. While Nguyen may not have done a lot of *traditional* promotion, he was running an amazing guerrilla marketing campaign.

Most casual games start out easy and get harder as you play. New players build mastery slowly, over time. Flappy Bird was different; beginners fail almost immediately. Every time you died, you saw this screen:

Game over? You can share your frustration on Twitter

The game's unexpected difficulty surprised people. It was unusual. Human beings have the desire to share things that are unique. Nguyen gave them an easy outlet to do this: the "Share" button.

I first heard about the game when popular YouTube personalities began featuring it in their videos. Soon after my friends started challenging me on Twitter to beat their score. It may have been unintentional, but Nguyen achieved the dream of every app developer: he got people talking about his game.

How to use this book

The first section of this book is called *Build Something People Want.* While it's aimed at developers who are still looking for an idea, the principles apply to every marketing stage.

Developers who have built a product, but haven't yet launched, should start with the *Lean Marketing Stack.* After that, continue to the section entitled *Before You Launch.*

The biggest part of the book is called *After You Launch.* It contains numerous tactics you can try once your product is public, with the aim of helping you get your first 100 customers.

Before we get started, I want us to be honest with each other. I've already told you my goal:

> *Help software developers earn an income from their projects so that they can gain more freedom and independence.*

What's your goal? We will explore that question in the next chapter.

Define your goal

Before you do anything else, you need to define *what* you want to achieve. Why do you want to learn marketing skills?

Here's how Aaron Vegh, a developer from Toronto, defines his "why":[3]

> *I'm a maker of software. I've been doing it for something like 15 years. Over the years, I've put together several apps for web, Mac, and iOS. Things that, to one extent or another, I've hoped to parlay into the ultimate freedom: to become independent, to earn more than I could make hourly, to have greater control over my own life.*

Your "why" is important because it will allow you to evaluate each project on whether it brings you closer to your goal. If one idea isn't gaining traction, you'll have the sense to stop working on it and move on to something else.

> *The key to getting things done is to understand why you're doing them.*

---

[3] aaron.vegh.ca/2015/08/im-looking-for-a-partner/

How to define your goal

Start small

Nothing kills momentum like a massive project that drags on for months. Are you building your first product? Make it something small. Shipping something small is better than not shipping at all.

Set a deadline

Give yourself a launch date. In this book, I recommend a three-month timeline, but you could make that window even smaller. Getting started is half the battle; finishing is the other half!

Put it on your calendar

Once you have your launch date, set aside regular time to work on your project. Getting up every Saturday at 6 am, and working 2 hours would be an effective way to build a habit. Once you're in a rhythm, it will be easier to get the work done.

Write it down

I write my goals in a text file. You might prefer a notebook. Others prefer to go public with their goals by writing them on their blog. Research done at the Dominican University of California has shown that writing your goals down improves your chances of achieving them.[4]

---

[4] www.dominican.edu/dominicannews/study-highlights-strategies-for-achieving-goals

Start now

You can't procrastinate your way to success. To build momentum, *take your first step.*

Product work isn't easy. It's going to take sacrifice:

> *"It takes sacrifice to make something great. To shift your mindset and experiment with ideas, you have to choose a new path. You have to change your paradigm from consumption to creation."*
> *– Paul Jarvis, Everything I Know*

To succeed, you're going to need to develop healthy habits. Get off Twitter, turn off notifications, and put yourself in a place where you can focus.

I can't guarantee that this book will help you achieve your goal.

Success is always a mixture of timing, knowledge, execution, and persistence. However, these pages will give you the knowledge you need. It's your job to bring the performance and endurance!

Now, let's get to work.

I

Build Something People Want

1

How to succeed

> *"If your product is remarkable, getting noticed is a lot easier."*
> *– Giacomo "Peldi" Guilizzoni, founder of Balsamiq*

Want to make marketing easier? Build the right product, for the right audience.

When something is truly exceptional, people talk about it. They want to share it with others.

Think about the last app you bought. Chances are, you heard about it from a friend, reviews in the app store, or on social media.

Great products generate worth of mouth.

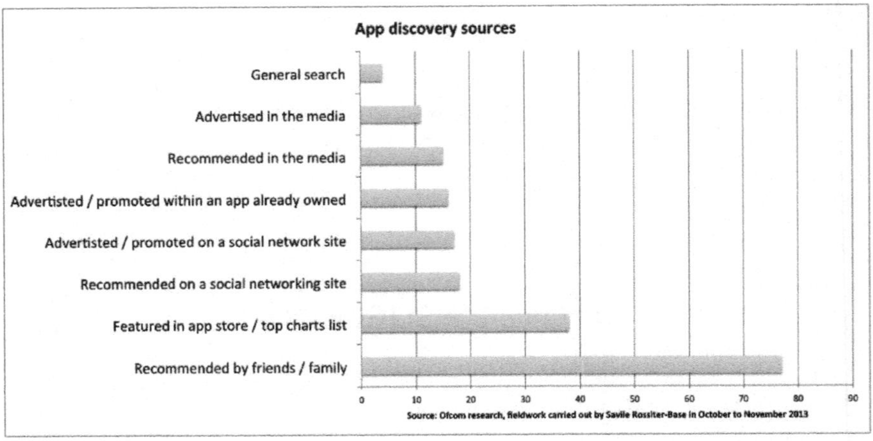

How do people discover new apps in the App Store?

Researchers at UCLA found that when we discover something new, our brains are wired to spread the news. Matthew Lieberman, a UCLA psychology professor, states here:

> *We always seem to be on the lookout for who else will find this helpful, amusing or interesting, and our brain data are showing evidence of that. At the first encounter with information, people are already using the brain network involved in thinking about how this can be interesting to other people. We're wired to want to share information with other people. I think that is a profound statement about the social nature of our minds.*

Ideas are risky

Years ago, I was watching an episode of *The Dragons' Den* on Canadian television. On the show, aspiring entrepreneurs pitch their products to wealthy investors.

At one point, a married couple (John and Peggy) came on stage. They were pitching a series of sports trivia booklets, the kind you might see in the checkout aisle of your grocery store. The investors asked John and Peggy a series of questions. In the midst of this questioning, an ugly truth emerged: they had been working on this idea for 11 years and hadn't yet earned a profit. Even worse, they had invested their entire life savings into the project.

Why had Jon and Peggy invested so much of their time and money into an idea that had so little traction?

There's a risk for creators like us to fall in love with our ideas. Sometimes we succumb to the sunk cost fallacy. We feel like we've invested so much time, energy, and money into our idea, that we couldn't possibly give it up.

If your goal is to achieve product traction, you have to be brutally rational about your idea. You can't put good marketing after a bad product and expect good results.

Does this story sound familiar to you?

It's 1 am, and you can't sleep. You have a brilliant idea, and you can't get it out of your head. After fidgeting in bed for an hour, you go down to the basement and start coding.

By 7 am you have a working prototype. You keep working on it evenings and weekends; creating new features, refining the design, and building out the billing system. Soon, the whole thing is ready for launch. You deploy it to production and wait for your first customers to sign up.

But the customers don't come.

You double check your analytics. Everything's working properly, but no one is showing up. At this point, you might feel like you have a marketing problem. It's much more likely that you have a *product* problem.

Notice how that whole story revolved around you: **you** had the idea, **you** built it, and **you** launched it. Who is missing from this picture?

The customer.

Ideas can be exhilarating and inspirational. Users don't care about your idea; they just want help with their problems.

Remember: inspiration doesn't always lead to great products.

Sometimes, we're inspired by technology:

- "I could build this on the Twilio API!"
- "I could learn that new CSS framework!"
- "I could use this new tool I just bought!"

Motivation can also come from our need to make money, to impress people, or to validate ourselves in some way.

Instead of being focused on the customer, we're focused on ourselves! We need to change our thinking. Want a profitable business? Make products that improve your users' lives.

A visit to the barber shop

Last year I was walking to the barbershop, and I started daydreaming about the ways technology could improve his business.

I thought about how I'd booked my appointment: I'd called him, and he'd looked at his calendar on the wall and told me what times he had available. "What an inefficient system," I thought. I began to create software (in my mind) that would eliminate these inefficiencies, save him hundreds of dollars a month, and increase sales exponentially. Then, I walked in to get my haircut and got a reality check.

The conversation went like this:

Me: "So, have you ever tried using scheduling software for your appointments?"

Barber: "Oh man, I've tried like ten of them. Terrible! They're all terrible."

Me: "Really? None were helpful. Why?"

Barber: "Almost all my bookings happen on the phone or by text message.

There's nothing I've found that's more efficient than looking at a paper calendar on the wall and finding an open slot on there. If I have to walk over to the computer, I've already wasted too much time. I have five-seconds to look and determine when I have a spare block. All the software I've tried just gets in the way."

With one conversation, I was able to save myself the misery of creating something that people didn't want. Instead of code first, I went to a potential customer first. The software I was planning in my head wouldn't help my barber, so I didn't build it.

The most important skill

The most important product marketing tactic you'll learn in this book is listening.

You're probably a fan of quantitative research: aggregate numbers that we can collect without human interaction. I'm a fan too! It's awesome to look at big data sets and be able to crunch the data and observe patterns.

At the beginning of the process, the most helpful data usually isn't quantitative; it's *qualitative*. The advantage with this type of data is you don't need much traffic to produce results; you can go out and listen to real people until you start to see trends.

> *"You can't track very much in the early days: you just don't have enough data. Typical "startup metrics" don't solve your core questions at the beginning: What is my target market? How can I get product-market fit? And most importantly, can I get anyone to pay for this?"*
> *- Lars Lofgren, KISSmetrics*

In the beginning, you have to answer three important questions:

1. Which markets am I uniquely positioned to serve?
2. Of those markets, which can I reach efficiently?
3. Are they motivated and financially able to pay for things?

All of this leads to the million dollar question:

> ***How can I make their lives better with software?***

Good marketing isn't about employing the latest growth hack. At its core, good marketing is correctly identifying a legitimate problem that people will pay you to solve.

2

Choose the right market

Here's a truth that doesn't get talked about much:

Some markets are bigger, easier to reach, and more eager to pay than others.If you're hunting for ideas, you should start in an environment that matches these criteria:

1. Customers are motivated to spend money to improve their lives.
2. You can acquire customers through affordable marketing channels.
3. The customer base is big enough to support your business.

Case study: Nathan Barry and ConvertKit

Nathan started ConvertKit in 2013, positioning it as "Email marketing for digital product businesses." During this time he specifically targeted beginners. Initially, he was able to grow to $5,000 in MRR (monthly recurring revenue), but a problem emerged.

"Beginner customers are more likely to churn," says Nathan. Churn refers to users who cancel their subscription. For a Software as a Service business churn is the enemy. If you're bleeding more customers than you're acquiring, your business can't grow.

At the beginning of 2014, a bulk of ConvertKit's beginner customers churned, and MRR dropped to $1,337.

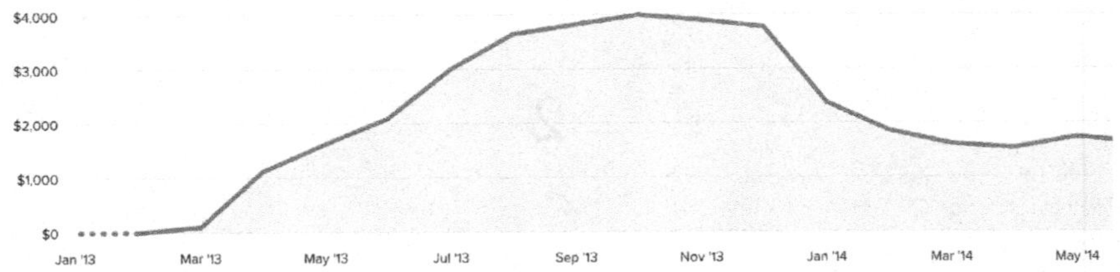

ConvertKit's MRR: January 2013 – May 2014

In October of 2014, Nathan made a big decision. He stopped working on all his other projects and went full-time on ConvertKit. The goal? Grow revenue and make the business profitable. He decided to change his target market from beginners to "professional authors." Nathan's full-time focus and new tagline helped! Revenue slowly began to grow again.

But ConvertKit's major inflection point came in March of 2015. Nathan decided to radically change the positioning from "Email marketing for authors" to "Email marketing for professional bloggers."

Other people in the industry made fun of him. "Really?" they said, "when are you going to target real businesses?"

However, the hunch paid off. In July of that year, revenue increased 48%. Growth continued from that point on. MRR went from $5,000 in 2015 to over $700,000 in 2017!

Nathan's story underlies an important point: target market and positioning play a significant role in a SaaS' success.

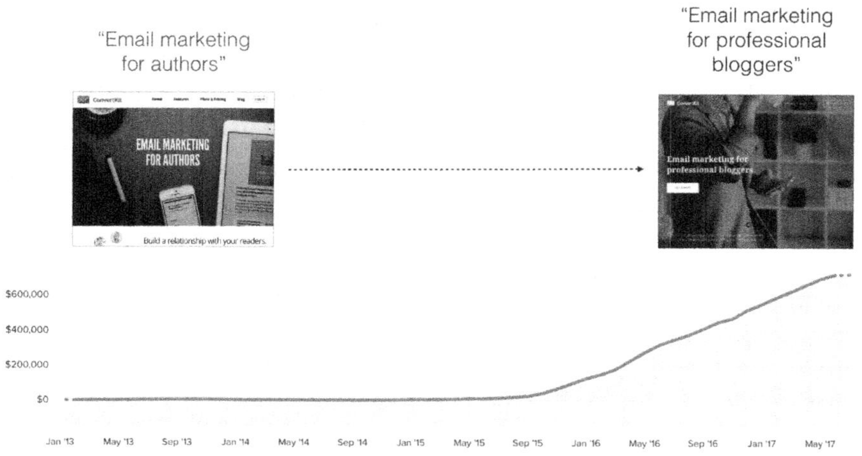

ConvertKit's MRR vs. positioning

"Positioning was key," Nathan later said, "we now serve one of the best markets in the world."

ConvertKit was improving their product along, but the real breakthrough came when they found their ideal customer.

> *"One of the truths of successful startups: the thing you set out to make is not usually what you end up making."*
> *– Fred Wilson*

How to find your ideal customer

There are two paths to building a profitable product:

1. Create your product first, and then find clients who want it.
2. Start with an excellent market, do your research, and make a product for them.

In this book, I recommend the second option. Here are some techniques for increasing your chances of choosing a profitable customer.

Start with people like you

Years ago, I met Mike McDerment from FreshBooks. FreshBooks is online invoicing software. Over 5 million folks use their platform to send invoices, accept payments, and track expenses.

Mike explained the genesis of FreshBooks in this blog post:

> *In January 2003 I was running a four person design agency. I was using Microsoft Word to create our firm's invoices, and I was pulling out my hair because Word simply wasn't built to create good looking invoices efficiently or report on my business. One day I accidentally saved over an old invoice, and something in me snapped – I knew there had to be a better way. Over the next two weeks I coded up a solution for my clients, and eventually, we turned that side project into what is now FreshBooks.*

I took a class from Mike on marketing strategies. He told us about all the different ways he was reaching potential customers. One thing stuck out for me:

> ***Me:*** *"Mike, it sounds like you're only going after web designers. Why not market FreshBooks to other niches?"*
> ***Mike:*** *"Starting with web designers made sense for us. We were designers, we knew where they hung out, we knew they were online, and we knew they needed to manage invoices (because we had that problem ourselves). It would have been way harder, and expensive, to go after plumbers. Web Designers was a niche we could easily get to."*

Since then, FreshBooks has expanded to serve all sorts of niches (lawyers, marketing agencies, therapists) but putting their initial focus on designers was key to their success.

Choose a market that is easy to reach

Mike also knew that web developers would be simpler to reach because they congregated in groups online.

In 2008 FreshBooks was running ads on TweetDeck and Echofon, two well liked Twitter clients. At the time, Twitter was still a relatively small network, made up largely of early adopters in the web community. It was the perfect place for FreshBooks to reach its niche.

Interest-based groups that congregate online are easier to connect than other types of folks.

I've consulted for multiple health startups whose biggest challenge has been to reach the medical doctors they wish to serve. The medical community is a closed community. They don't maintain social media accounts, and getting their email is challenging. These companies had to resort to cold calling and direct mail to reach their audience, which is significantly more expensive.

Find a market with buying power

You're looking for a customer who can buy your product easily. In Nathan's case, a professional blogger is the only person he needs to persuade to buy his product. There's only one decision-maker; they don't need to run their expenses by anyone else.

Many software products, like project management software, have to convince a whole team of people to make a sale. You need to talk to the CTO, the COO, the Product Manager, and the development team. Purchasing decisions made by committee increase the cost of every sale.

Purchasing power also refers to how much money people can spend to solve their problems.

A college student might have the autonomy to spend their money as they please, but they're generally cash poor. A business owner, on the other hand, has both spending authority and the budget.

Look for a market that has the desire to improve

You want the type of customer that is highly motivated to solve their problems. They're willing to spend money to overcome obstacles and make progress in their lives or their business.

Professional bloggers make most of their money by building an email list. They are a great market for ConvertKit to target because email is the core of their business. Furthermore, if they're having problems with their existing service (like MailChimp), they'll be highly motivated to switch.

Desire is important. Certain types of business owners can spend money as they please, but they're cheap. They're not willing to pay to overcome certain types of problems. If you've ever been a part of a business' budget discussions, you'll notice that every business has certain non-negotiables. Phone service, website hosting, and email service are necessary for most businesses. But other applications are just "nice to have."

Pick a market that's "big enough."

To have a sustainable business, you need enough people in your target market with the ability and desire to pay you. If your market is too niche, it's going to be difficult to make a profit. However, if there are thousands (or millions) of people in that market, your opportunity to attract leads is greater. Choosing a niche is still important, but it has to be sizeable enough to support your business.

For example, my friend Adam Wathan wrote a book called *Refactoring to Collections*. It shows PHP developers how to use Laravel Collections to refactor their code.

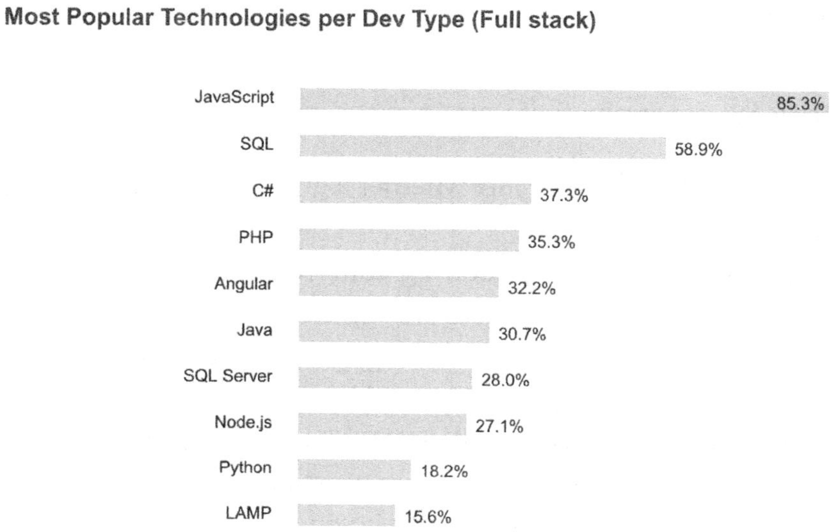

Stack Overflow Developers Survey, 2017[5]

Adam's potential market size is much greater than someone who focuses on Python programmers. He had another advantage: PHP was sizeable and was being ignored by many publishers. They felt it wasn't "cool enough." These developers were hungry for good resources.

A trick for choosing the right market

Ask yourself this question:

> *Who is already paying you for your time and expertise?*

My friend Francois was a web development consultant. Over time, he started attracting a specific clientele: Shopify store owners.

Eventually, he built a SaaS specifically for this group. They were already paying him as a consultant, so he knew they were likely to pay

---

[5] insights.stackoverflow.com/survey/2017

him for software.

A trick for determining if you have the right market

Here's a good way to evaluate whether a given customer type meets all these criteria.

If a market has a long-running conference or trade show, it's probably a safe bet. Conferences are expensive ($500+) and require a significant mass of people who are highly motivated to attend.

Look at Nathan Barry's audience of "professional bloggers." The BlogWorld conference (now called NMX) has been running since 2001 which attract hundreds of conference goers every year.

The other benefit of events like this is you can register, and get a feel for attendees. Ask them questions:

- What tools do they pay for?
- What's the most recent software purchase they made? What triggered that purchase?
- What are they currently struggling with in their business?
- What workarounds are they using? (what tasks are they currently doing in Excel?)

Do you like them?

Another good reason to attend conferences, events, and meetups: you'll get a sense if you like the customer.

Before rushing to create a product you need to stop and ask: "Do I even want to serve this market?"

There's a lot of advice on finding product/market fit. My recommendation is that you get founder/market fit right first.

> *"Product/market fit is a* ***good market*** *with a product that can satisfy that market." – Marc Andreeson*

When Marc says "good market," he means a defined group that can pay for products.

By that definition, dentists are a lucrative market. They run profitable businesses. They're willing to pay to save time, save money, or make money. But just because they have problems to solve, doesn't mean you're the person to solve them.

My friend Patrick McKenzie had that experience. He used to run a SaaS called Appointment Reminder. Before launching, our mutual friend Peldi asked him a question:

> *"Is optimizing the schedule of dentists' offices your passion?"*

When Patrick answered "no," Peldi was exasperated:

> *"Then why are you committing to working on that for the next several years?!"*

Serving an audience, you don't like is one of the worst feelings in the world. You have to show up every day and answer their emails, fix their bugs, reset their passwords. To do customer research, you need to hang out with them a lot. Want to get sales? You have to go to trade shows, make contacts, call them on the phone.

> *Put another way: if you don't like cats, don't start a feline rescue center.*

Why product/founder fit matters

In September 2015 Marco Arment woke up to discover he had the #1 paid app in the App Store. He'd developed an early ad blocker for iOS called Peace.

He'd previously achieved success with other apps, like Instapaper and Overcast, but nothing to this level.

He should have been ecstatic; but instead, he was miserable. He described his inner conflict on his blog:

> *Achieving this much success with Peace just doesn't feel good, which I didn't anticipate, but probably should have. I still believe that ad blockers are necessary today, but I've learned over the last few crazy days that I don't feel good making one. Even though I'm "winning," I've enjoyed none of it. That's why I'm withdrawing from the market.* ***I'm just not built for this business.***[6]

Here's another example of why product/founder fit matters:

I was at a conference when I met Chris. He'd spent his whole life in the lottery business. He noticed a huge opportunity: China and India were just getting into legal gambling. He'd just inked deals worth millions of dollars. He asked me if I wanted to join him.

I thought about it. I could see the potential: Chris had a product that governments overseas needed and wanted. Getting to that market first has huge advantages.

I declined the offer.

For me, gambling just doesn't fit. Working on a lottery product doesn't match my values. I don't gamble, or play games at all. The money was attractive, but I couldn't see myself working on it every day. It's just not right for me.

I'm not saying we should only build products that are "exciting." A lot of apps are boring and unsexy. That's OK. The key is to solve problems for a group of people you're passionate about. If you can make money doing that, without undermining your values, you're winning.

---

6 marco.org/2015/09/18/just-doesnt-feel-good

Market checklist

Selecting a target market for your software product is one of the most important decisions you'll make. Evaluate each potential market with this checklist:

- Are you familiar with this market? Have you worked with them before?
- Is the market easy to reach?
- Do they have the ability to pay for products?
- Do they have the desire to improve themselves / their business?
- Is the market big enough?
- Would you like to have them as customers?

3

Understanding Jobs to be Done

Jobs to be Done (JTBD) is a theory for understanding what motivates customers to buy your product.

People want their lives to be better. They have a vision of where they want to go. But there are obstacles in their path. Customers hire products to help them move forward; to make progress towards their vision of a better life.

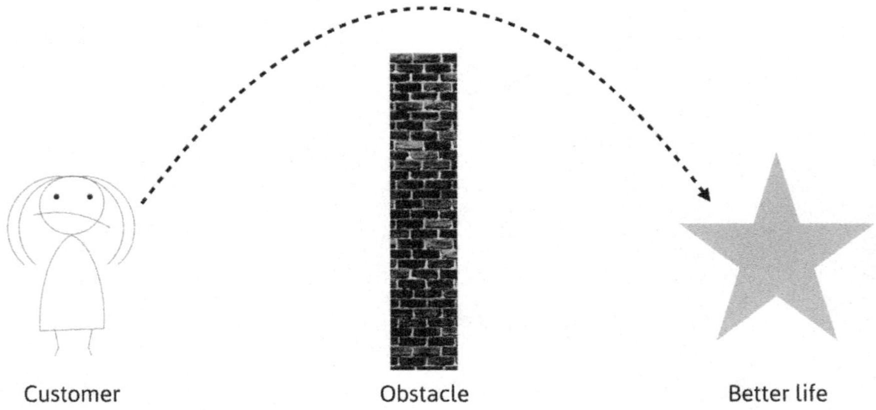

You can think of it this way: users "hire" software to help get their job done. My friend Alan Klement defines it this way:

> *"Customer + Product = Progress"*

Building successful products isn't just about creating a ground-breaking technology! As Clayton Christensen explains in his book, Competing Against Luck:

> *The word "progress" might not spring to mind when you're trying to innovate. Instead, you obsess about creating the perfect product with just the right combination of features and benefits to appeal to customers. You think you know just what your customers would like, but in reality, it can feel pretty hit or miss. Place enough bets and, with a bit of luck, something will work out.*

Jobs to be Done helps you understand why a user might hire your software to get their job done.

Who is using it?

Companies like Intercom and Basecamp have made big bets on JTBD and made it a part of their product development process.

Jason Fried, of Basecamp, reported that interviewing their customers generated valuable product insights:

> *What's most interesting is the situations people find themselves in before they're our customers. It's not about this industry or that one. It's not about demographics, either. It's not even about the competitive set, yet. It's all about the situation they're in, the reality they're trying to wrangle, and the progress they're trying to make.*[7]

Describing a job to be done

Here's an example of how Freshbooks might define their JTBD:

---

[7] signalvnoise.com/the-why-before-the-why-c5492520acf0

Free me from the agony of creating and tracking invoices manually so that I can get paid faster.

Alan Klement has three criteria for defining a JTBD:

1. Make sure you're not describing a task or activity. It's not about getting a drill so you can drill a 3/4" hole. It's about how your life gets better after you use the drill: hanging a beautiful painting and having your friends admire it.
2. Describe how the customer has solved that job in the past, and how they might solve it in the future.
3. Understand what motivates the customer. How will things be better for the user when they overcome the struggle?

How do you figure out the JTBD for your product? You'll need to get a deeper understanding of the customer's journey and their motivation for change.

Seeing the customer journey

Understanding the initial trigger, and the events that lead up to the purchase will help you design an effective marketing strategy for your product.

You can visualize the process like this:

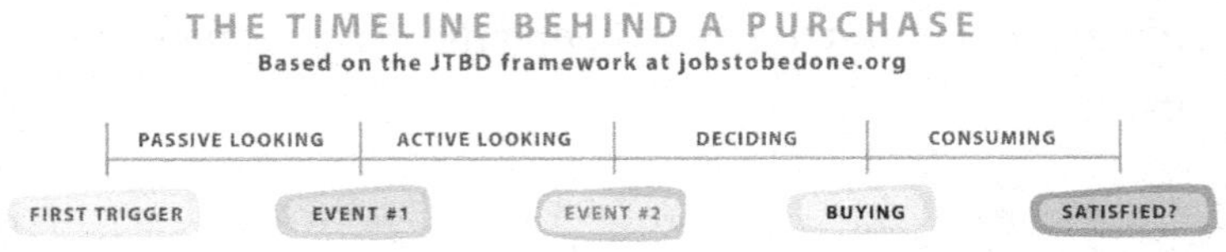

Back in 2012, I was a Product Manager. I convinced my team that we should use Sprintly as our project management software.

But how did that happen? How does someone go from not hearing about a product to buying it?

Here is the timeline of events:

- **May 2011:** the SaaS I was working for decided to adopt Scrum for our team. We hired a consultant to get us started. Soon after, we stopped using Basecamp and started using Pivotal Tracker as our project management tool.
- **June 2011:** My boss saw Joe Stump speak at FOWA. He raved about the talk, especially Joe's line: "Starting a business is really, really, really fucking hard."
- **January 2012:** I saw that there was an episode of TWIST with Joe Stump. I'd remembered my boss had liked his talk at FOWA. I listened to it on the way to work and heard about Joe's new company: Sprintly. I believe I signed up for a trial account.
- **February 2012:** During this time, the CTO and I were getting frustrated with Scrum. It just didn't seem to fit our team's workflow. I started reading about the benefits and flexibility of the Kanban philosophy.
- **April 2012:** During my Kanban research, I started googling for "kanban project management software." One result that came up: a blog post by Joe Stump about Sprintly's digital Kanban board.
- **May 2012:** Pivotal Tracker was getting harder for us to use: again, it just didn't feel like it matched our team's workflow. I invited our CTO to my trial Sprintly account and floated the idea of switching. We decided to use Sprintly and Pivotal at the same time, to see if we liked it.
- **June 2012:** The CTO and I decided that we wanted to switch to Sprintly. We championed the idea to the rest of the team, sold them on it, and started paying for Sprintly.

As you can see, my exposure to Sprintly starts with my team adopting Scrum. Over the next 13 months, numerous events eventually lead us to the "hiring" event, when we signed up for a paid plan.

Understanding the customer's JTBD will help you optimize how people discover (and eventually buy) your app. In my example, I was looking for a way to make Scrum easier to implement in our team. I tried hiring Basecamp and Pivotal Tracker for the job, but they fell short. Eventually, I found Sprintly, which gave me the progress I wanted.

How can you use Jobs to be Done?

Customer interviews

One way to understand someone's Job to be Done is to interview them.

Alan Klement has written an excellent guide on conducting interviews, with sample questions you can ask.[8]

He recommends starting with these questions:

1. When did you purchase the product?
2. Where were you?
3. What time of day was it? (daytime/ nighttime?)
4. What was the weather like?
5. Was anyone else with you at the time?
6. How did you purchase the product?
7. Did you buy anything at the same time?

If you don't yet have a product, you can ask a competitor's customers these questions.

The interviewee's answers will help you understand the context of the actual buying decision.

[8] jtbd.info/a-script-to-kickstart-your-jobs-to-be-done-interviews-2768164761d7

Observation

Aside from interviews, you can also observe people making purchasing decisions, both in-person and online.

Folks often leave clues on social media, in forums, and in blog posts, that help us understand the timeline behind a purchase.

Here's an example from Twitter user @dakotaw:

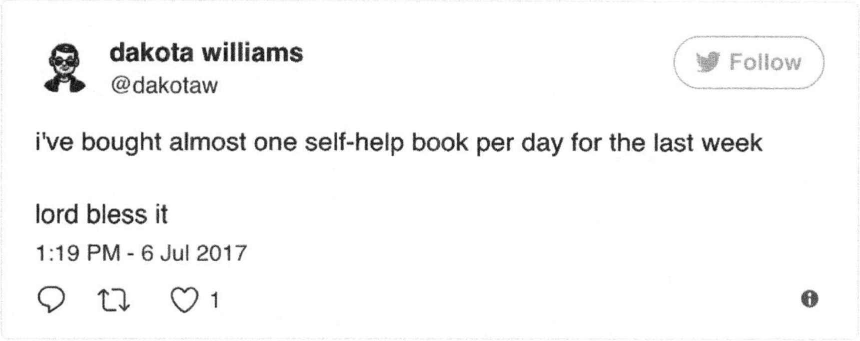

He mentions he is buying a new book almost every day. Five days later he tweets this message:

In this case, buying a lot of books serves as a trigger to consider the Kindle Unlimited service.

How would we define Dakota's JTBD?

> *"Give me unlimited digital books so that I can read more self-help books."*

What else could Dakota hire to get this job done? Kindle Unlimited isn't his only option. He could also hire:

- The public library
- Audible audio books

Kindle Unlimited also competes with anything else that might attract Dakota's attention: Netflix, podcasts, and college courses.

Optimize for the job to be done

In 10+ years of doing product marketing, I haven't found a better framework for understanding why people buy software.

JTBD shows us that we're not in the business of making products, we're trying to make super humans. In the words of Kathy Sierra[9], the purpose of a product is to make a "badass user:" your app should give users abilities they never had before.

You can use JTBD principles to observe human beings and gain two valuable insights:

1. How do they want their life to be better?
2. What obstacles stand in their way?

Once you understand this, you build products that help people improve their lives. You're not guessing; you're delivering the progress they desire.

It's crucial that you organize all of your efforts around helping users make progress. Whether it's marketing, coding, or customer support, everything should contribute to their forward movement.

JTBD is particularly useful when you're deciding which features to build. Think about what John Palmer is saying here:

> *"Jobs to be Done does not describe what the product must do; it describes what the customer must do."*

A new feature should give your user the ability to do something they weren't able to do before.

For example, I use Canva.com to design book covers, podcast art, and header graphics for blog posts. Previously, I had to hire a designer to do those things. It was costly and slowed me down.

But now, with Canva, I have a new superpower: I can design assets myself. We might describe the JTBD like this:

> *"Give me the ability to do design work myself, so that I can publish my work sooner (without waiting for a designer."*

More resources

I've just scratched the surface of the Jobs to be Done theory.

To dig in deeper, I recommend:

- *When Coffee and Kale Compete,* a book by Alan Klement
- *Competing Against Luck,* a book by Clayton Christensen

4

Research

Why research your audience?

Understanding your customers' struggle is key to building software they want.

The case studies and data you collect will also help you with your promotion. Anecdotes from your audience will inform the headlines and marketing copy you write on your website.

> *"If you can describe the problem better than your customer they will assume you have the solution."*
> *- Pat Flynn*

People have a dream of a better life. What stands in their way? Obstacles. They hire products to help them overcome those hurdles.

The purpose of doing research is to uncover customer desires. Finding an idea that people will pay you for is challenging. Patrick McKenzie highlights this here:

> *"If you're not targeting one of the top two most pressing issues in my life, I'm not going to buy your thing."*

To market your product, you will need to figure out what your audience desperately wants.

The research process

The research phase follows these steps:

1. **Determine who your audience is**, and where they hang out.
2. **Collect data** by observing people online and doing interviews. This could be on Twitter, on forums, or on sites like Quora. You're looking for frequently asked questions and common pain points.
3. **Prune the data.** Go through your data and find patterns. Get rid of the outliers, and find the results that come up repeatedly. The question you're trying to answer is: "What is a struggle that needs to be solved? Where are they getting stuck?"
4. **Create a hypothesis**: what is the most relevant problem?
5. **Test your hypothesis**: offer a small fix for their problem and observe how they respond. You could provide a 7-day email course, a little software tool, or a one day workshop. Judge the response by how many people sign up.
6. **If your test is successful**: continue adding value. If not, go back to step 2.

In the last chapter, we covered the first phase (finding your audience). Next, you'll need to research your audience to discover what they *want*.

Unearth the struggle

To find a problem worth solving you need to recognize patterns. It takes time to hone this skill, but with practice, you'll learn to do it intuitively. Hang out with your audience and keep your eye open for reoccurring themes.

Having an audience that congregates online is an advantage because they're easier to observe. You can read their interactions in comments, forum threads, and interchanges on Twitter. When you do this every day, week after week, you should start to see some patterns.

Coffee example

Let's pretend "coffee snobs" is our audience. Where would we find this type of coffee drinker?

Reddit. This is a good place to start because there are subreddits for *everything*.

Sure enough, when I go to reddit.com/r/coffee in my web browser, this pops up:

> *Well, you do love coffee right? Why else would you be here? It turns out that /r/coffee loves coffee too. In fact, I think we all love coffee! So let's talk about it here. The world of coffee is more complex than just a tasty caffeinated beverage to get you going. This is a place to talk about the farms, the beans, the baristas, the roasters, the industry, the brewing gear and your specially tuned brewing techniques. It's a place to ask questions about how to make your daily cup just a little bit better. It's a place to learn, share and make new friends. Welcome to /r/coffee!*

Next step: hang out. Log in every day, and listen. What are the reoccurring themes?

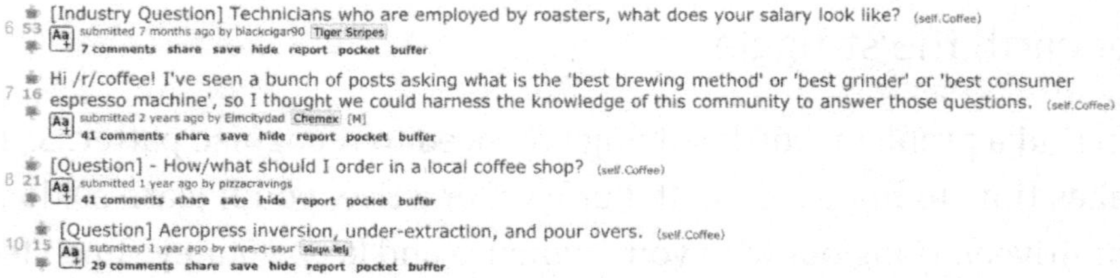

What are your audience's top questions?

Bookmark the themes you see repeatedly. You can use a tool like Pocket or Keeeb to do this. In Keeeb you can even drag and drop the snippets you've saved into different groupings.

After you've collected data over a period of 3–6 months, trends will emerge. In the case of coffee, the predominate pattern might be: *How do I build a pour over stand?*

Prune your data so that the real insights emerge. Remove the outliers and focus on the topics that seem to be getting the most traction.

Write your hypothesis

Once you've pruned your data, you'll write your theory about what customers want:

> *Help me build a pour over stand so that I can impress my coffee snob friends.*

Put this on paper and look at it. Do you believe it? Is this your audience's biggest desire? Go back to your notes and look at all the supporting evidence you collected. Once you're sure, move on to the next step.

Prove your hypothesis

It's not enough to *have a theory;* you need to test it! Here are a few methods for testing whether you've struck a legitimate pain:

Landing page with call-to-action

To ensure that you've hit the right nerve, create a landing page that highlights the pain. My friend Jarrod Drysdale did this beautifully with this page at thetinydesigner.com.

Jarrod Drysdale's "Tiny Designer" landing page is an excellent example of validating a hypothesis

At the end of this page, he put a call-to-action (CTA) asking people to sign up for a free 5-week email course. Offering a free resource and asking for an email address is a good method for gauging interest. If many people download your free guide, you know you're onto something.

Another example of this is Sean McCabe. He's a designer and illustrator who loves creating and drawn letters. Sean decided to create a free guide for other people that wanted to learn hand lettering. He was surprised by the reaction: over 100,000 people gave him their email to download the PDF. Riding that momentum, he created an online course called Learn Lettering. His launch was a success because he'd been able to target a particular need he saw in his community.

Find ten people who say they'll buy

Ultimately there's only one way to ensure that your product idea is good: will people pay money for it?

Finding customers is often the last step in our product development process. We think: "First I'll come up with the idea, then I'll build it, and then I'll go find people who want to buy it."

That process is backward. It's better to bring your idea to people and ask if they'd pay for it. You could present it to them as a landing page, a press release, or a working prototype. Even better: offer them a solution *right now* by solving their pain manually.

It's important to ask them for a commitment: "If I built this would you pay for it?"

Jason Cohen, of WPengine, advocates going even further and getting a cheque from them right there.

Success! Go forth and build

Once you've confirmed that you've found a "job to be done," it's time to make the initial version of your product (or feature, if you're expanding on an existing product).

5

Target the struggle. Paint the dream.

> *"Everyone hates X and wants it to be easier."*

That simple formula is how my friend Adam Wathan finds new product ideas. He was having a hard time writing maintainable CSS, so he made a CSS framework.

Adam likes working in public, and will occasionally livestream his coding sessions. He kept getting feedback from viewers that CSS was their biggest struggle. They were interested in learning Adam's approach.

When Adam created a landing page for his CSS framework, it got 1,100 subscribers in less than 18 hours.

Remember that line I quoted in the previous chapter? Mike McDerment was discussing why he started building FreshBooks:

> *"I was using Microsoft Word to create our firm's invoices, and I was pulling out my hair because Word simply wasn't built to create good looking invoices efficiently or report on my business."*

He could have created many things for the web design community: portfolio software, a set of Photoshop filters, or inspirational posters for their walls. Instead, he chose the most frustrating and pressing problem he faced: creating, sending and tracking invoices. It wasn't the sexiest or most technically challenging problem to solve, but it was an issue that was making him pull out his hair in frustration.

There is an advantage of choosing an audience that you belong to; finding problems to solve gets easier.

If you've been a developer for 16 years, why would you try to build a product for lawyers, real estate agents, or retail store owners? Think about how many hours of practice you've put into learning the field of software development. It would be difficult for a lawyer to build a product for developers. He doesn't have the domain expertise he needs to compete.

The same is true for you, as a developer. If you choose a market you know nothing about, the odds are stacked against you.

The servant's mindset

A product person is a servant. Instead of thinking about themselves, they think about their customers: "What do they need? How can I help them?"

Building and marketing a product is less like being Steve Jobs, dramatically sharing your wares from a stage, and more like a tow-truck driver, rescuing someone with a flat tire.

B2B markets are lucrative because there are plenty of businesses who need roadside assistance. They need help with software, with design, with project management, and with finances. They need someone (that's you) who can build them a product that will get them back on the road, in better shape than they were before.

Find their most urgent problems and solve those first; like an emergency dispatch center prioritizing 911 calls. Also, businesses are willing to pay more to address critical problems.

Types of struggle

Your marketing approach will depend on how much discomfort the customer is in!

> *"One thing that people don't appreciate enough is that there are different types of pain."*
> *- Patrick McKenzie, on the Product People podcast*[10]

Before you start building your product, ask yourself: how intense is the pain I am targeting? The severity of the customer's struggle will determine:

- How much they are willing to pay for the solution
- How desperate they are to find a solution

To explain, I'm going to ask you to think about your dentist (stay with me).

Your dentist deals with different thresholds of pain:

- **Extreme pain**: "ARGH! This toothache is killing me! I need a dentist right now!!!"
- **Moderate pain**: "My gums have been bugging me lately. I should book an appointment sometime soon."
- **Low pain**: "I haven't gone in for a checkup yet this year."

(I also like the way Michael Buckbee defines pain intensity. He asks: "Does this pain need morphine, aspirin, or a vitamin?")

There will always be some problems that people just won't pay to solve. If people perceive the problem to have a low pain threshold, there's little you can do to convince them otherwise. I once owned a snowboard shop in my suburban hometown. One of my marketing campaigns was to get people "buying locally." I was trying to target a

---

[10] productpeople.tv/2012/12/26/patio11-part2/

pain people didn't have. They were happy to drive 15 minutes to the big city to buy snowboard equipment, and get a better price and more selection.

Notice how the marketing your dentist employs corresponds with the intensity of the pain:

Extreme pain (morphine)

The customer is highly motivated to find a solution. It's urgent! They google "dentists nearby" and book an appointment with the first office that has availability.

In a situation like this, search engine optimization (SEO) and search engine marketing (SEM) would be the primary focus. This is "pull marketing": the customer is desperate and in motion. They're under pressure to find a solution quickly, which is why having good page rank (or an ad at the top of the screen) makes sense.

Businesses targeting *extreme pain* also have a pricing advantage. Often, the greater the pain, the more people are willing to pay (this is why Uber can use surge pricing).

What are some examples of products that solve *extreme pain* points?

- Zapier: "If we don't figure out this integration this week, we're going to lose this deal."
- JSON-CSV: "My developer went home for the day, and I need to convert this JSON data to a CSV right now."
- Churnbuster: "How am I going to deal with all the customers with expiring credit cards?"

Moderate pain (aspirin)

Advertising for "moderate" pain-points should employ both "push" and "pull" techniques.

For example, the dentist might place an ad in the paper that says,

"Experiencing gum discomfort? We can fix that!"

Pull-marketing proactively reminds the customer that there is a solution for their problem.

Push-marketing occurs when something in a customer's life motivates them to seek out a solution. For example, the Google search "how to get rid of gum pain" is evidence of a painful situation.

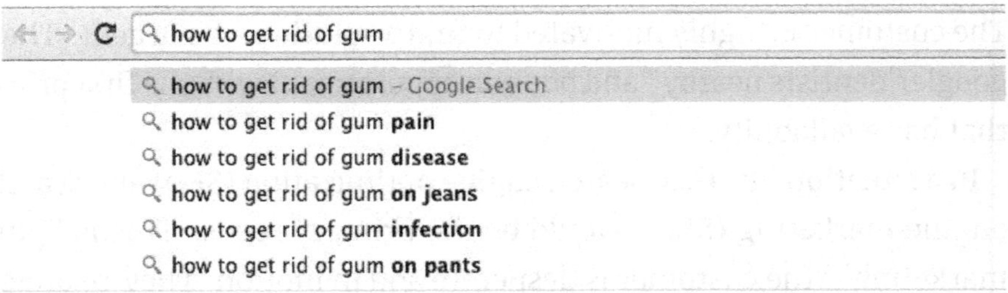

What are people searching for in Google?

There is an opportunity to solve moderate pain points, but it's also where many entrepreneurs fail. Finding a pain that people will pay to get rid of isn't easy.

> *"You want people who know they have the problem and who are actively looking for solutions, rather than a pain that's bearable."*
> *- Patrick McKenzie*

What are some use-cases where products solve *moderate pain* points?

- Baremetrics: "I wish I didn't have to update this Excel sheet manually with our SaaS numbers every month."
- Slack: "There's gotta be an easier way to communicate with my team than email."

Low pain (vitamin)

What do I mean by "low pain"? These are problems that require more of a vitamin, than aspirin.

These solutions require **a lot** of pull marketing. The company needs to both show the consumer that they have a *problem* and then persuade them to buy their *solution*.

Your dentist's office spends a considerable amount of its budget reminding you to come in for regular checkups. They'll send you a postcard every six months, and follow up with phone calls, just to get you to book that appointment.

Most people don't wake up in the morning and think: "I should call my dentist today." Getting you to book that appointment requires an outside *pull*.

Here are some examples of web products that solve *low pain* points:

- Stamps.com: "Going to the post office is annoying."
- Squarespace: "My brother-in-law keeps bugging me to build him a website."

If you listen to podcasts, you know that Stamps.com and Squarespace spend a considerable amount of money trying to get you to visit their websites. This is pull marketing at play. If you're selling a vitamin, you're likely going to need big marketing dollars to make sales.

I have a theory: there's an inverse relationship between the level of pain and the number of exposures a customer needs before he buys.

As an example, the distribution could look something like this:

- **Extreme pain:** 1–2 exposures
- **Moderate pain:** 3–7 exposures
- **Low pain:** 8–100+ exposures (much harder to forecast)

In advertising, they call this *effective frequency*. There are many theories around optimal frequency (some say three, others say seven is the magic number).

However, there is some evidence that supports my theory:

- Indochino (low pain) bumped up its retargeting frequency from 3 impressions per user per day to 15-20. "Every time we've increased it, we've seen greater revenue and ROI."
- When ReTargeter did a study on conversions per impression, they found that B2B (high pain) ads outperformed B2C (low pain) ads by 402%. "There tends to be a higher sense of purchase urgency with business solutions than with consumer goods."

It's not enough to find a pain point and build a solution. You have to remember that different types of pain will require different marketing approaches.

If you're marketing an **extreme pain** solution, focus on SEO and SEM.

Moderate pain products require a full-spectrum of tactics. You'll use pull marketing (ads, retargeting, content marketing, PR), as well as push marketing (SEO, email courses).

If you're planning on building a **low pain** product, remember that you'll likely need a big marketing budget. The only low-cost acquisition strategy here is "viral," and that is extremely difficult to get right. Historically, there have been opportunities in SEO to secure low competition, high traffic keywords, but those are increasingly hard to find.

Jeremy Hageman makes a good point about pain frequency: some pains reoccur daily (commuter traffic), while others may only be experienced once a year (income taxes).

Also: pain points move up and down the continuum: what requires morphine today might only require an aspirin tomorrow. There are all sorts of factors that can affect this: improving technology, increased competition, the changing behaviors and values of customers. Most successful B2B products have both "extreme pain" and "moderate pain" use cases, and they market to both.

Product first, marketing second

In this section, we've looked at the importance of building something people want. You can't put good marketing after a bad product and expect good results.

Now that we've laid this foundation, it's time to build your marketing machine.

II

The Lean Marketing Stack

6

Overview

What is the Lean Marketing Stack?

The *Lean Marketing Stack* is the base infrastructure you'll need to market your product. It includes three fundamental tools:

1. Your website
2. Basic analytics
3. Your email list

Why are we setting this up now? First: the sooner you can start collecting data, the better decisions you'll be able to make. How will you know if your campaign is a success if you don't have any metrics?

Second: there's always a chance that your product will get traction *before* you expect it. I've spoken to hundreds of developers who had their product featured on Hacker News or Product Hunt before they were ready. They had no way to track conversions or have people sign-up for a waiting list. Don't miss out on these opportunities!

Third: building a basic website forces you to answer important questions. These include, "Who is my product for?" and "Why should they care about my product?" Writing a simple landing page helps focus your product development on *what users want*.

How much will this cost?

If you're looking to save money, you can use these providers and pay nothing:

- **Website hosting:** GitHub Pages, Tumblr
- **Analytics:** Google Webmaster Tools, Google Analytics, Mixpanel
- **Email list:** MailChimp

In this chapter, we'll cover the basics of setting up the *Lean Marketing Stack.* If you'd like to set up more detailed analytics, read the chapters that follow.

Your website

If you don't already have a website for your product now is the time to build one. It doesn't need to be fancy, expensive or take a long time to create. A simple landing page will do to start.

Domain set up

Are you building a web application? My recommendation is to organize your domain structure like this:

- **yourname.com** - marketing site
- **app.yourname.com** - production server for your web application
- **staging.yourname.com** - staging server for your web application

Keeping your marketing site separate from your app will help keep your visitor data clean: it delineates between your app's users and people visiting your marketing page.

If you haven't found a good domain name yet, tools like Hover and Lean Domain Search offer great name recommendations.

Content Management System or plain HTML?

I'm a fan of both! If you're going to start blogging right away, use a content management system (CMS). Otherwise, a static HTML site will work fine.

If you're hosting a simple static site, I highly recommend GitHub Pages. You host your files directly from your GitHub repository; when you push your changes, they go live on the web. Also, GitHub provides you with its global Content Delivery Network, for free.

Which content management system should I use?

I've worked for large consulting companies and small startups, and almost all of us end up using WordPress. It's a great CMS for marketing sites. It's flexible, has great integrations, and you can host it almost anywhere.

Do not manage the hosting yourself! A premium hosting service like WPengine or Pagely might *feel* expensive but will save you hours of administration time. Site Ground is another good option and is less expensive.

If you'd rather not use WordPress, consider trying Squarespace. It's powerful, simple to use, and starts at $8 per month. For the speed of a flat-file CMS, and the power of the command-line, use Jekyll.

Another good free option? Tumblr! You can add a custom domain at no cost, there are many cool themes available, and it has a great blogging engine.

Thinking about hosting is one of the rabbit holes that developers fall into. *Yes, you could probably do it yourself, cheaper and better.* As a product creator, your most valuable asset is your time. If you can save time by hiring an existing tool, you should!

Site design

Marketing sites built by developers have a telltale design: they use the default Bootstrap theme. As a developer, fiddling around with a design isn't the best use of your time. Here are some useful resources for site templates:

- **HTML themes:** Wrap Bootstrap, ThemeForest
- **WordPress themes:** Launch Effect, ThemeForest
- **Other options:** LeadPages, Unbounce, Squarespace, Levels Landing Page, Carrd

The goal here is to communicate *who* your product is for and *how* it solves their pain. Once you're making sales, you can invest more money into your marketing site. In the meantime: keep it simple!

Analytics

Marketing is about testing, analyzing the data, and iterating. To do this well, you're going to need metrics that tell you *who* is buying and *why*.

First step: set up Google Webmaster Tools

At one point, Google's webmaster tools were only marginally helpful. Nowadays, it is the only place to see which search terms people are using to find your site. You should install this right away because the more data it collects, the sooner you'll get valuable results.

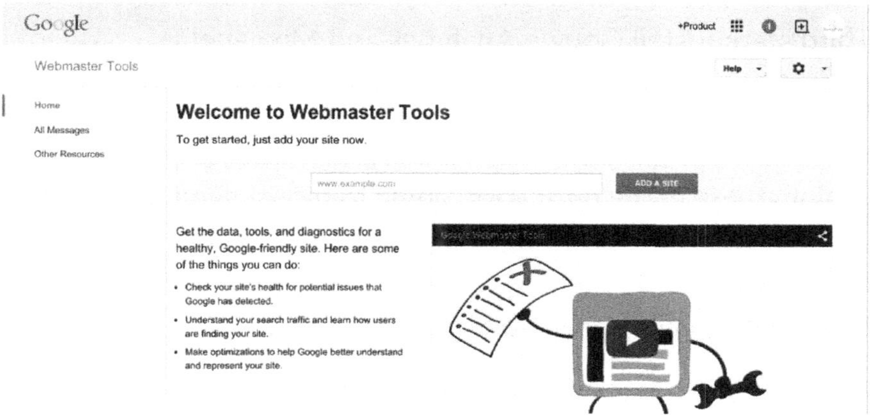

Second step: install Segment

Every time I'm on a project and skip this step, I end up regretting it. Segment describes themselves as "a single hub to collect, translate and route your customer data." It allows you to add new tracking snippets to your site without having to go in and change your code each time.

It also stores your historical event data and automatically loads that data into the new tools you choose. Now, instead of interacting with multiple APIs, you only need to work with Segment's.

> ***Note:*** *if you tried Segment in its early years and were disappointed I'd recommend trying them again. They've solved their data leakage and latency issues.*

Their free tier for developers will give you up to 100,000 API calls a month, perfect for a new project.

For a detailed explanation on how to set up tracking events in Segment, go to the next chapter.

Third step: install Google Analytics and Mixpanel

Once Segment is recording events, you can configure other integrations. For analytics, Segment features over 38 tools. While you can explore these in the future, I'm going to recommend that you start with Google Analytics and Mixpanel. Both of them are free (Mixpanel has a free tier for developers) and both cover the essentials you'll need for tracking goals, funnels, and cohorts.

Fourth step: A/B testing (optional)

If you already have a site that's generating more than 5,000 unique visits per month, you may want to try some basic A/B tests.

> *"The single highest ROI tactic which I know of for software companies is conversion optimization. Unfortunately, the overwhelming majority of you aren't doing it."*
> *- Patrick McKenzie*

Traditionally, split testing tools have been costly. Optimizely used to have a free Starter plan that gave users basic functionality (and up to 50,000 visitors per month). At the time of writing, that tier had been replaced by a 30-day free trial. If you have the time, and interest, I think it's worth signing up.

To install Optimizely, sign up for an account, and then put their tracking script just below the opening <head> tag of every page you want to track.

Your first test

You need to start somewhere! When your landing page is up, install the Optimizely script and create an initial experiment.

Make it simple! Start by testing one variation of your main *headline* and your main *call-to-action*.

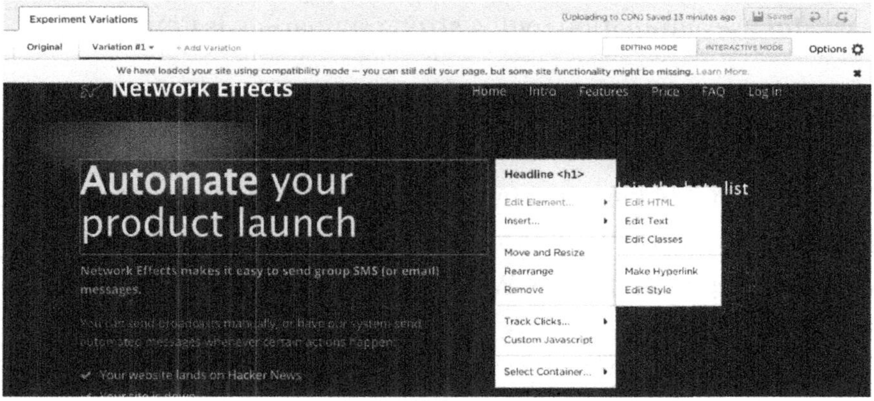

This will give you a baseline for future tests. There are two types of goals I track in A/B tests:

1. **Conversions:** who went through the process of signing up for your mailing list or buying your product?
2. **Clicks:** what did visitors click on while they were on your page?

Optimizely gives you a default goal called "Engagement." I usually disable this goal, as it tries to measure general interaction on the page, which feels like a fuzzy metric.

Last step: mailing list

Nathan Barry once told me: "My email list is my most important asset." Most people will visit your website and leave, but if you can get their email address, you'll have additional opportunities to contact them.

We'll talk about setting up email forms, squeeze pages, and drip sequences later on, but for now, let's talk about choosing an email provider.

In this book, I'm recommending you use MailChimp. It's free for up to 2,000 subscribers, has many built-in integrations, and features an easy-to-use automation tool. A strong runner-up is ConvertKit.

Those are the basics

If you're about to launch your product, I recommend reading the following chapters. Here, I'll explain how to set up more detailed tracking events in Segment, Google Webmaster Tools, Google Analytics and Mixpanel.

7

Setting up Segment

Segment is software that manages all your integrations. It's also an important part of our marketing stack: it tracks the user data that we'll feed into Mixpanel, Google Analytics, and Optimizely.

The benefit to you, the site owner, is you only have to install the JavaScript snippet and tracking events once. Once installed, you can add new integrations using the Segment UI.

Here is the other benefit: each time you enable a new integration, it will automatically use your historical data from Segment.

Step 1: Sign up and install the JavaScript snippet

Start by going to segment.com and signing up for an account. They'll first ask you to define a username for your account. After that, they'll help you set up your organization's account (in your case, your "Organization" is your team). Finally, they'll get you to set up a project. For Segment, a project is a web app, mobile app, or an individual website.

After you sign-up, create a personal account and define your organization, you'll be asked to create a project

To install tracking on a website, you'll use Segment's Analytics.js. They'll provide you with a snippet that looks like this:

```
<script type="text/javascript">
!function(){var analytics=window.analytics=window.analytics||[];if(!analyti
analytics.load(" 000-YOUR-API-KEY-000 ");
analytics.page()
}}();
</script>
```

The write key lets us send your data to the right place.

Install the Segment script in the header of your site

Once this snippet is installed on all your relevant pages, you'll able to use the Google Analytics integration right away. For all the other integrations, you'll need to identify users, plus track pages and events.

Worried that Segment will affect your page load times? Don't worry! Analytics.js loads asynchronously. The page won't wait for Segment and its integrations to finish loading before showing the page to visitors.

Step 2: Create a tracking plan

A tracking plan is a list of the events you want to track. The best place to start is by defining your funnel.

For example, mine looks like this:

- Viewed homepage
- Signed up for email sequence
- Viewed registration page
- Signed up for account

In Segment, these are the categories you'll use:

- **Events:** these are user actions you'd like to track. Examples: *Logged In*, *Logged Out* and *Signed Up*. This is also where you'll track events such as *Mailing List Sign Up*.
- **Pages:** which pages are users viewing in your funnel? Some

examples: *Homepage*, *Blog*, and *Mailing List Confirmation*.

- **Screens:** if you have a mobile app, you can identify the different screens users are viewing. Examples: *Sign Up*, *Main Menu* and *Settings*.

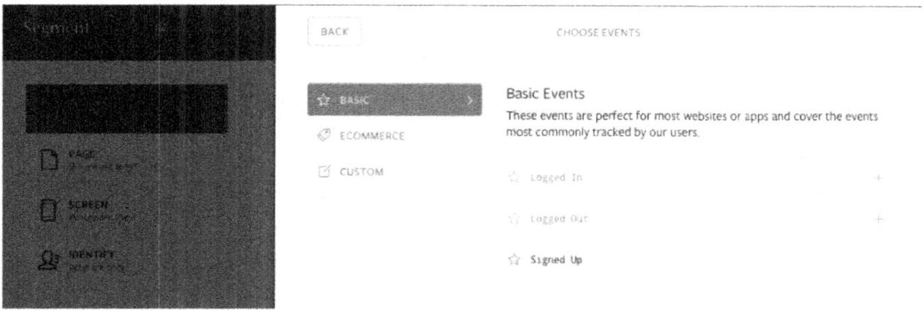

Use Segment's Tracking Plan feature to plan out everything you'd like to track in your funnel.

Step 3: Identify users

As a default, when a new person visits your site, Segment will treat them as an *anonymous visitor*. The next step is to correctly identify that person after they've signed up for an account or signed up for your mailing list. Once Segment's identify method is called, it will associate all of their anonymous history on your site with a particular user identity.

Here's what a basic identify call would look like in JavaScript:

```
analytics.identify({
email: 'string',
first_name: 'string'
});
```

If you're creating a course or membership site on WordPress, you can use Segment's WordPress plugin. This will automatically identify users and registrations.

You can view user traits in the "Identify" section of the Schema menu:

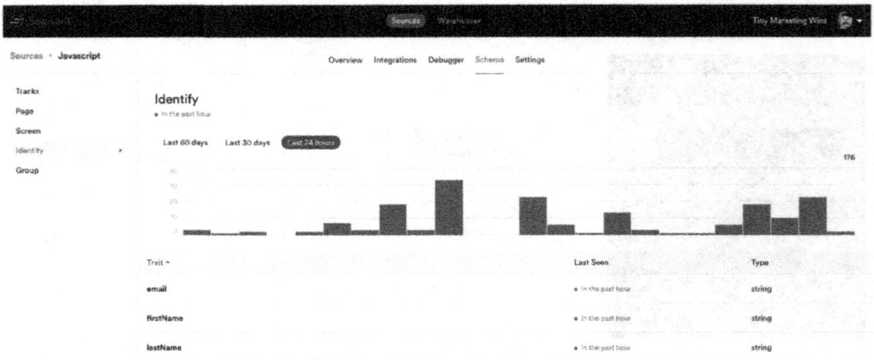

Step 4: Add code for tracking events and page views

Now it's time to enact your tracking plan. Go back to the placeholders you created earlier under *Events* and *Pages*.

Note: if you're using the WordPress Plugin, you can get by without having to install any code manually. Just ignore this section!

Events

Let's start with events. These are the actions people will be doing on your website or in your app. They could include things like: *Subscribed to Newsletter*, *Logged In*, and *Created Item*.

Segment will give you code samples in JavaScript, .NET, Ruby, Java, Android, PHP, Python, Node, iOS and GO. Here's what the Newsletter tracking event would look like in JavaScript:

```
analytics.track('Subscribed to Newsletter');
```

Add all your event code to the appropriate places on your marketing site, and in your app.

You can also add properties to your events. For example, if you allowed people to log in via GitHub, your event call might look like this:

```
{
"type": "track", "event": "Logged In", "properties": {
"accountType" : "GitHub"
}
}
```

Pages

Tracking which pages people are viewing will allow you to build funnels and follow their progress through your marketing site and into your product.

A very common page to track is your *Homepage*. For that, you would include *analytics.page("Homepage");* in the snippet you're loading on the homepage:

```
<script>
...
analytics.load("PNgy1f94eYd3h91XiTaHdDM5BsnCjsGq");
analytics.page("Homepage");
}}();
</script>
```

Once you've saved this page, visit it in your browser. You should see the *Page* show up in the Segment debugger.

If you click on the event, you'll get more detailed information about the call. Here's an example:

```
analytics.page('Homepage', {
name: 'Homepage',
path: '/',
referrer: 'https://www.google.ca/',
search: '', title: 'Network Effects',
url: 'http://networkeffects.me/'
});
```

Example: Mailing list set up

Let's say you want to identify people who come to your landing page and sign up for your mailing list.

Your code could look something like this:

```
<script>
jQuery(document).ready(function($){
```

```
analytics.track('Viewed Subscription Form');
$("#mailing-form").submit(function(e){
var form = this;

// Stop form from submitting too early
e.preventDefault();

var fname = $("#first_name").val();
var email = $("#email_address").val();

analytics.track("Subscribed to Newsletter", function(){
analytics.identify(email, {
email: email,
first_name: fname
}, function(){
$(e.target).unbind('submit');
form.submit();
});
});
});
});
</script>
```

Now, if you tested this (by submitting the subscription form) you would see something like this in Segment's debugger:

```
analytics.identify('marketingfordevelopers@bizbox.ca', {
email: 'marketingfordevelopers@bizbox.ca',
first_name: 'George'
});
```

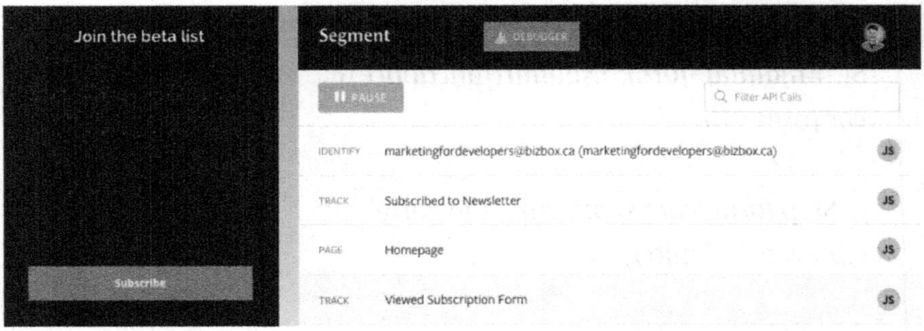

You can test this tracking event by performing the action, and seeing if it shows up in the debugger

If you have other integrations enabled in Segment, you'll see this data in other apps as well. For example, here's how the registration above would look in Mixpanel:

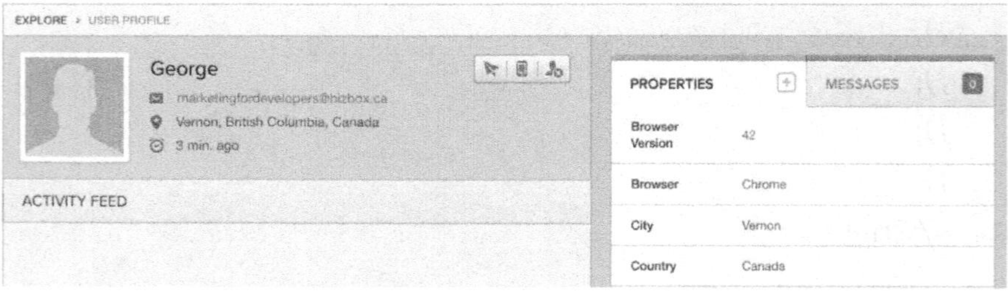

The user's data is sent to your other integrations, like Mixpanel

The pieces are in place

You have successfully installed the Segment tracking code that identifies people who are visiting your site, follows the pages they view and tracks the events (actions) they take on those pages.

Now, it's time to put this tracking to good use in Google Analytics, Mixpanel, and Optimizely.

8

Using Google Webmaster Tools

Webmaster Tools has always been in the shadow of Google's much larger Analytics tool. However, there's some hidden functionality in here that you can use to track the effectiveness of your search engine optimization work.

Tracking search queries

The SSL conundrum

In 2011, Google implemented secure search (https://google.com) as a default for all users. Search Engine Land explained what this change meant for site owners:

> *When someone searches Google, it is now always done as an SSL encrypted search, so all search queries are now encrypted. It routes the click to the website through a redirect so that the website a user lands on has no idea what actual keywords the searcher found the website under, and what keywords were used that brought the person there.*
> *- September 30, 2013*

When using Google Analytics, you could no longer see organic keywords (the terms people were using to find your site).

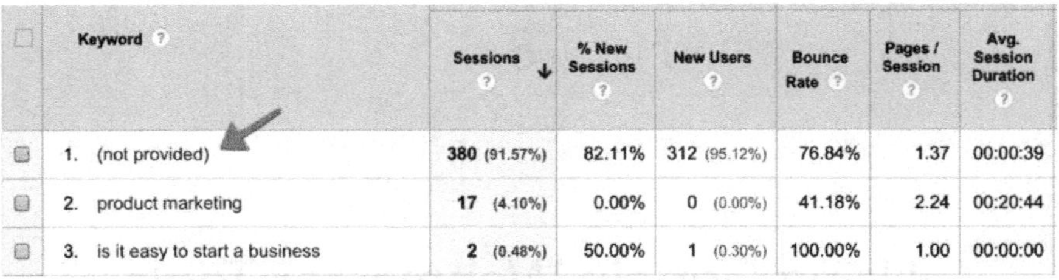

	Keyword	Sessions	% New Sessions	New Users	Bounce Rate	Pages / Session	Avg. Session Duration
	1. (not provided)	380 (91.57%)	82.11%	312 (95.12%)	76.84%	1.37	00:00:39
	2. product marketing	17 (4.10%)	0.00%	0 (0.00%)	41.18%	2.24	00:20:44
	3. is it easy to start a business	2 (0.48%)	50.00%	1 (0.30%)	100.00%	1.00	00:00:00

Google no longer provided organic keywords in Analytics

Webmaster Tools to the rescue

Here's a secret: you can find your keyword data in Google's Webmaster Tools. Go to google.com/webmasters and then navigate to *Search Traffic >> Search Analytics.*

You can now find keyword data in Google Webmaster Tools

This new report, introduced in May 2015, provides a more accurate picture of search data. Broadly, for Queries, it will provide these metrics:

- **Queries:** which Google search queries show your site.
- **Clicks:** the number of clicks for that query (people who clicked on your search result, and visited your site).
- **Impressions:** how many times your search result was viewed in a Google search.
- **CTR (Click-through rate):** this is the percentage of clicks divided by the number of impressions for that query.
- **Position:** this is the average position of your site on Google search results.

Along with Queries, you can group your data by Pages (individual pages on your site and how they rank), Countries, Devices (desktop, mobile, or tablet), and Search Type (web, image, video).

How to use this data

First, your site will need to have some history for Search Analytics to be helpful. If you haven't been writing blog posts, creating landing pages, and accruing inbound links there won't be much to show here.

Once your site is indexed by Google and is ranking for a few keywords, the data in Search Analytics will become more useful. Here are the questions you should be asking of your data:

1. **For which search queries is my site ranked 1–5?** Finding out where your pages are ranking high will help you double-down on queries that are working well. Put out more targeted content aimed at these keywords. These could be landing pages or blog posts that illustrate how your product answers that query.
2. **For which search queries is my site ranked lower, 9–15?** You can improve your position for these queries! The queries here should provide you with ideas for new content: blog posts, landing pages, and articles. Include the query's keywords inside the title

of your new page. This approach should help you rank higher for these queries.

3. **Which queries are giving me the most impressions?** You'll see that certain keywords get far more views than others. Focus on those!
4. **How many click-throughs am I getting?** The most important metric is how many people are visiting your site from these search queries. Look for ways you can improve your click-through rate.

Grouping by *Pages* and filtering by click-through rates can be particularly helpful in learning what types of content people are searching for on Google.

	Pages	Clicks ▾	Impressions	CTR
1	/words_japan.html	555	12,365	4.49%
2	/	441	11,363	3.88%
3	/blogs/	362	3,685	9.82%
4	/words.html	360	12,642	2.85%
5	/vika-byske-standing-desk/	345	3,769	9.15%
6	/remote/	343	10,832	3.17%

Group by Pages to see which pages have the highest CTR

You'll also want to watch for dips and spikes. These could be due to a crawl error (Google can no longer find a page on your site), or an algorithmic penalty (Google has tweaked their ranking algorithm, and your site is being penalized.

Each year, Google changes its search algorithm around 500–600 times. While most of these changes are minor, Google occasionally rolls out a "major" algorithmic update (such as Google Panda and Google Penguin) that affects search results in significant ways.

- Moz

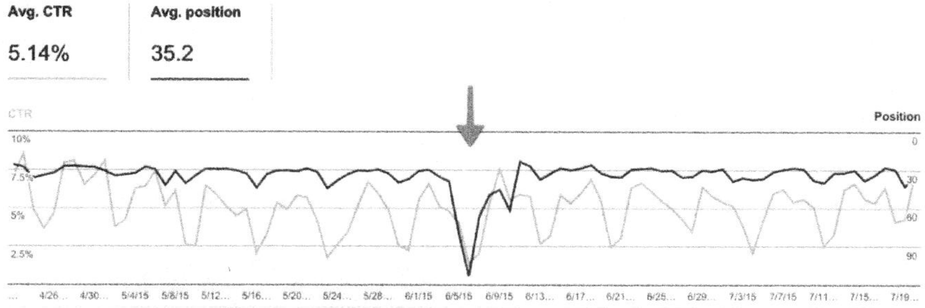

Use Search Analytics to watch for dips and spikes

Is your site mobile friendly?

In November 2014, Google started adding a "Mobile Friendly" label to search results that rendered correctly on mobile devices.Helping user find mobile-friendly pages, November 18, 2014

The next year, in April, Google also announced that sites that were not mobile friendly would be penalized by their ranking algorithm.Finding more mobile-friendly search results, February 15, 2015

You'll want to ensure that your marketing site is mobile friendly. Google has built a utility into Webmaster Tools[11] to do that.

The utility will show you how their Googlebot sees your web page and whether it passes their mobile test. If your page does not pass, it will tell you why and give you steps to remedy the problem.

[11] google.com/webmasters/tools/mobile-friendly/

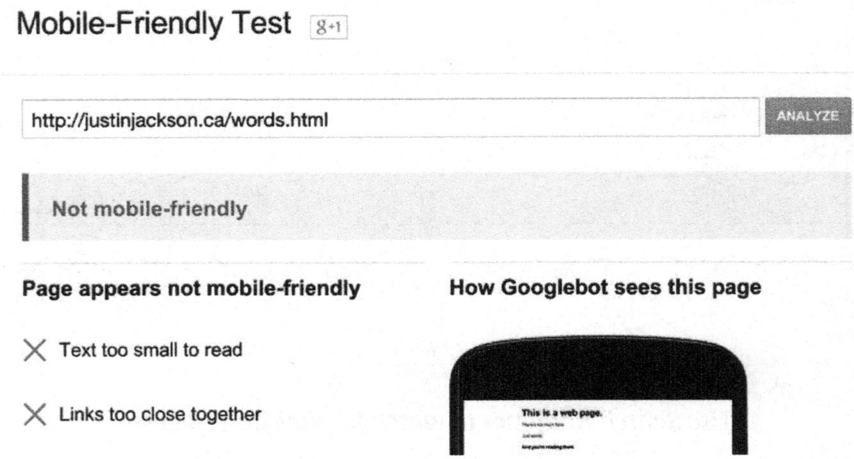

Google's Mobile-Friendly Test

If your pages aren't mobile friendly, it might be time to update your site's design. Take a look at *The Lean Marketing Stack: Overview* chapter for recommendations on good site templates.

9

Using Google Analytics

Google Analytics is confusing

However, there are a few places where it shines:

1. **Tracking Visitors and Visits:** if you want to see traffic numbers, especially in real-time, go to Google Analytics first.
2. **Tracking Bounce Rate, Time on Page, and Exits:** again, Google Analytics' strength is in visitor analytics. It's easy to get data on bounce rate, how much time people have spent on particular pages, and at what point they're leaving your site.
3. **Tracking Referrals:** it's helpful to know where your traffic is coming from! Google Analytics provides useful referral data, plus email alerts so that if you get a spike from a particular source, you'll know right away.

UTM tracking

Adding UTM codes to your URLs allow you to track different campaigns in Google Analytics. You may have seen URLs with UTMs in the past. Here is an example:

> *http://devmarketing.xyz/?utm_content=buffer9d562&utm_medium=so-*

cial&utm_source=twitter.com&utm_campaign=buffer

This one came from Buffer, a tool I use to share links on social media. When someone clicks on that link and comes to my site, Google Analytics will analyze it like this:

- **Medium:** social – *Describes the type of traffic. Examples: email, social, cost per click ads.*
- **Source:** twitter.com – *This is a label for where the traffic is coming from. Examples: search engine, newsletter name, Facebook, Twitter.*
- **Campaign:** buffer – *Identifies the slogan, product name, or promo code for this campaign.*
- **Content:** buffer9d562 – *The* ***content*** *tag is used to track multiple links when they point to the same URL.*

Creating UTM links

You can craft these URLs by hand, but most folks use Google's URL Builder.[12]

The bigger challenge is managing all the URLs you've created. I recommend using a spreadsheet to keep track of each URL. It should look something like this:

	A	B	C	D	E	F	G	H	I
1	UTM Tracker								
2									
3	Date	Website URL	Source*	Medium*	Campaign Name*	Term	Content	Final URL	
4	7-Dec-15	http://devmarketing.xyz	tinymarketingwir	email	tiny_day12			http://devmarketing.xyz?utm_source=tinymarketingwins&utn	
5	7-Dec-15	http://devmarketing.xyz	tinymarketingwir	email	tiny_day11			http://devmarketing.xyz?utm_source=tinymarketingwins&utn	
6	7-Dec-15	https://gum.co/devmarketingcom	tinymarketingwir	email	tiny_day10			https://gum.co/devmarketingcomplete/tinymarketing?utm_sc	
7	7-Dec-15	http://devmarketing.xyz	tinymarketingwir	email	tiny_day10			http://devmarketing.xyz?utm_source=tinymarketingwins&utn	
8	7-Dec-15	http://devmarketing.xyz	tinymarketingwir	email	tiny_day8			http://devmarketing.xyz?utm_source=tinymarketingwins&utn	
9	7-Dec-15	https://gum.co/devmarketingcon	tinymarketingwir	email	tiny_day8			https://gum.co/devmarketingcomplete/tinymarketing?utm_sc	
10	7-Dec-15	https://gum.co/devmarketingprer	tinymarketingwir	email	tiny_day8			https://gum.co/devmarketingpremium/tinymarketing?utm_so	

A copy of this UTM Tracker spreadsheet is included with this book

[12] support.google.com/analytics/answer/1033867

Generate your campaign URLs in this spreadsheet, and they'll be saved for future use. This will ensure you don't accidentally tag a campaign using the wrong variable names (i.e., blackfriday vs. black_friday).

Viewing UTM data in Analytics

If you regularly generate UTM links for your site, you'll be able to filter by the Medium, Source, and Campaign variables in Analytics and create reports like this:

Campaign	Sessions ↓	% New Sessions	New Users	Bounce Rate	Pages / Session	Avg. Session Duration
1. buffer	**146** (53.09%)	56.85%	83 (44.86%)	76.03%	1.33	00:00:35
2. guest_posts	**89** (32.36%)	79.78%	71 (38.38%)	89.89%	1.15	00:01:09
3. facebook_ads	**17** (6.18%)	76.47%	13 (7.03%)	88.24%	1.00	00:00:33

Report that shows visits filtered by Campaign

UTM information is particularly helpful in these reports:

- Acquisition > All Traffic > Source/Medium
- Acquisition > Campaigns > All Campaigns
- Conversions (you can filter by Source / Medium and Campaign)

If you're doing a good job of tracking all your ad, social and content campaigns with UTM tags, you'll be able to see which campaigns, sources, and mediums convert the best.

Viewing real-time stats

Want to know who's on your site right now? Head over to the Real-time report and observe which referrers, social sites, or keywords are sending traffic, and which countries people are visiting from.

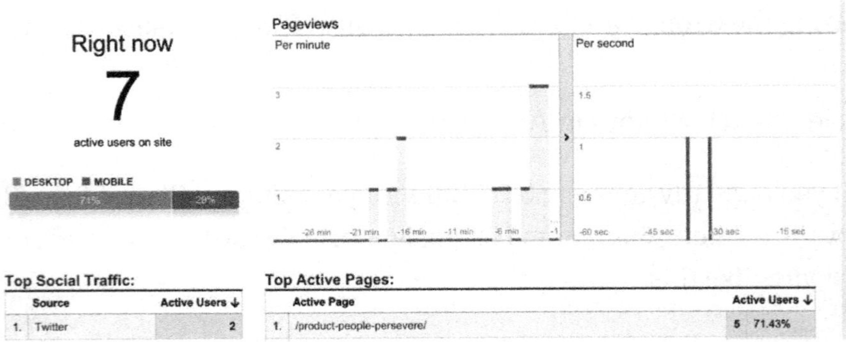

This report is particularly helpful if you notice a big influx of traffic and want to figure out where it's coming from. It also gives you immediate feedback: send out a tweet, and you can see how much traffic it generates.

Acquisition

To start, the only chart you'll want to pay attention to under Acquisition is the one you'll find under All Traffic >> Source/Medium.

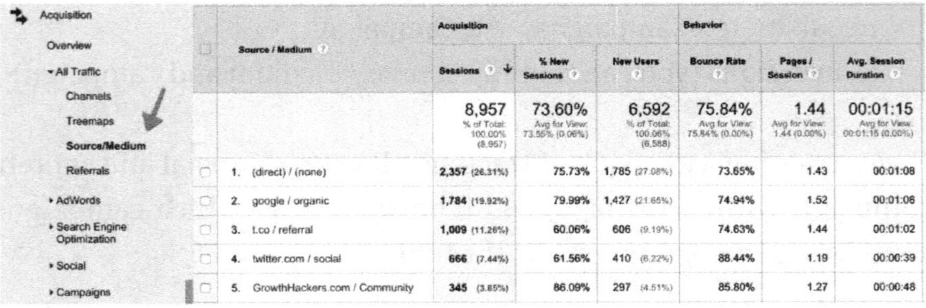

Source / Medium	Acquisition: Sessions	% New Sessions	New Users	Behavior: Bounce Rate	Pages / Session	Avg. Session Duration
	8,957 % of Total: 100.00% (8,957)	73.60% Avg for View: 73.55% (0.06%)	6,592 % of Total: 100.06% (6,588)	75.84% Avg for View: 75.84% (0.00%)	1.44 Avg for View: 1.44 (0.00%)	00:01:15 Avg for View: 00:01:15 (0.00%)
1. (direct) / (none)	2,357 (26.31%)	75.73%	1,785 (27.08%)	73.65%	1.43	00:01:08
2. google / organic	1,784 (19.92%)	79.99%	1,427 (21.65%)	74.94%	1.52	00:01:06
3. t.co / referral	1,009 (11.26%)	60.06%	606 (9.19%)	74.63%	1.44	00:01:02
4. twitter.com / social	666 (7.44%)	61.56%	410 (6.22%)	88.44%	1.19	00:00:39
5. GrowthHackers.com / Community	345 (3.85%)	86.09%	297 (4.51%)	85.80%	1.27	00:00:48

The *Source* side will describe which site the traffic originated from (google.com, twitter.com). The *Medium* side will show what kind of traffic it was:

- **Organic** - unpaid search traffic from Google
- **CPC** - Cost per Click advertising, paid search traffic from Google
- **Referral** - traffic from other websites
- **Email** - traffic from emails
- **None** - direct traffic (or unknown source)

Behavior

The oddly named *Behavior* report is an appraisal of your site's content. When people talk about "vanity metrics" they're often talking about stats in this section, because they focus on pageviews.

See your site's most popular content

If you want to see your site's most popular content, sorted by pageviews, go to *Site Content >> All Pages*. You will see total *Pageviews* in the second column, and *Unique Pageviews* in the third. *Unique Pageviews* only count a single pageview per visitor.

Setting up Goals

You have goals for your website. You want people to:

- sign up for your newsletter
- create a trial account
- buy a T-shirt

- download your app
- fill out your contact form

When you drive traffic to your site, *your goal(s)* is how you evaluate success. Google Analytics has a reporting feature (conveniently named Goals) for just this purpose.

To get started with Goals, follow these steps:

1. Log into Google Analytics
2. Click on the *Admin* link in the top menu
3. In the third column (far right), click on *Goals*
4. Click the red *New Goal* button

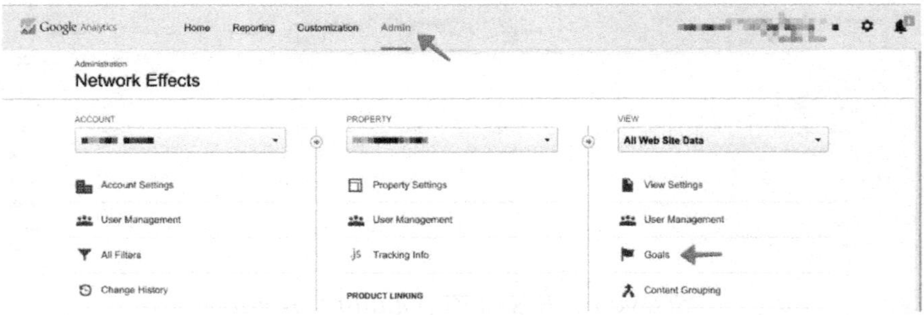

To find Goals, click Admin in the top menu, and Goals in the menu on the far right

Next, in your *Goal setup*, you'll be able to choose a pre-made template (*Reservations, Make a payment, Make an appointment*) or choose a *Custom* setup. Most often I choose *Custom*.

After that, you'll define the *Goal description* and *type*. There are four types to choose from:

- **Destination:** a site URL you'd like to track when viewed. Example: a confirmation page like /thank-you.html for email sign-ups.
- **Duration:** an amount of time you'd like to target. Example: 10 minutes.
- **Pages/Screens per session:** the number of pages you'd like to

target. Example: 4 pages.

- **Event:** a particular action performed on your site. Example: played video.

Example: newsletter sign-up

Is increasing newsletters sign-ups important to you? In this case, your Goal would look like this:

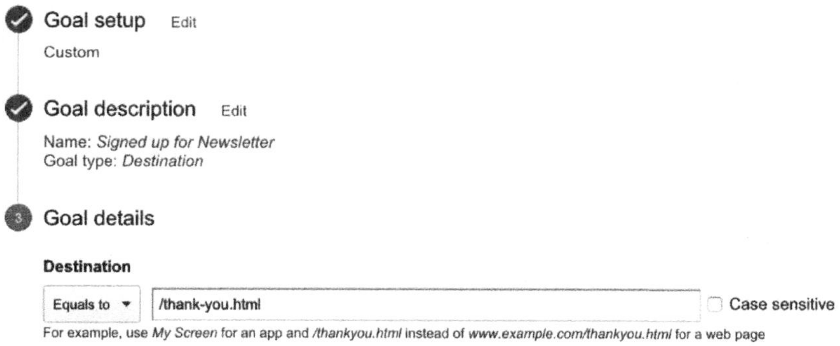

Goal: get visitors to sign up for newsletter

Note: don't worry if your Goals don't verify right away. In the above example, I knew I'd tested the destination page twice, but when I verified it, Google said the Goal had a 0% conversion rate. When I came back the next day, it had recorded my test visits.

> *"I've noticed this as well. Google's goals don't tend to update for up to 24 hours."*
> *- Mike Taber, The Single Founder Handbook*

Now that we've set up this Goal, we can track it in Analytics. Here's an example of my test visits:

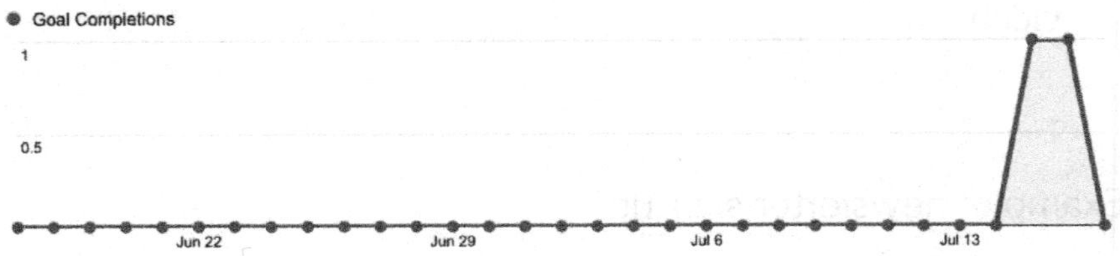

If you've set up your Goals correctly, you'll start to see results in your Reports

Setting up a funnel

Creating a funnel

A funnel describes the steps it takes the user to get your Goal. Typically, you only use funnels in situations where customers are giving you money.

Although I prefer to track these in Mixpanel, you can also set up funnels in Google Analytics. You may want to do this to save money (if you move beyond Mixpanel's free tier) or to compare Mixpanel's results to Google's.

To set up a funnel, go back to *Admin >> Goals* and edit your Goal. Flip the switch that says *Funnel* to on. Now, enter in the steps users will typically take to get to your goal. Don't worry; these don't have to be in exact order.

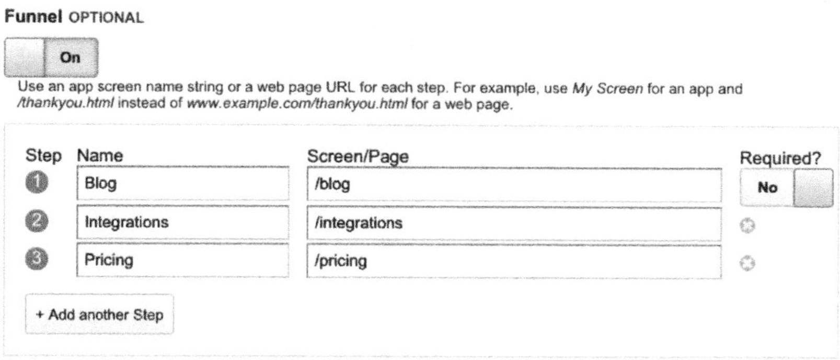

Here's an example funnel for a SaaS product

Viewing a funnel

To view your funnel, go back to the *Reporting* tab and click on *Conversions >> Goals >> Funnel Visualization* or *Goal Flow* in the side menu.

> ***Go to sleep:*** *if you're sure you've set everything up correctly, but Google's showing a blank funnel, it probably hasn't collected enough data. Turn your computer off and wait until tomorrow!*

You'll see each step of your funnel, and where you're losing people. The funnel view looks like this:

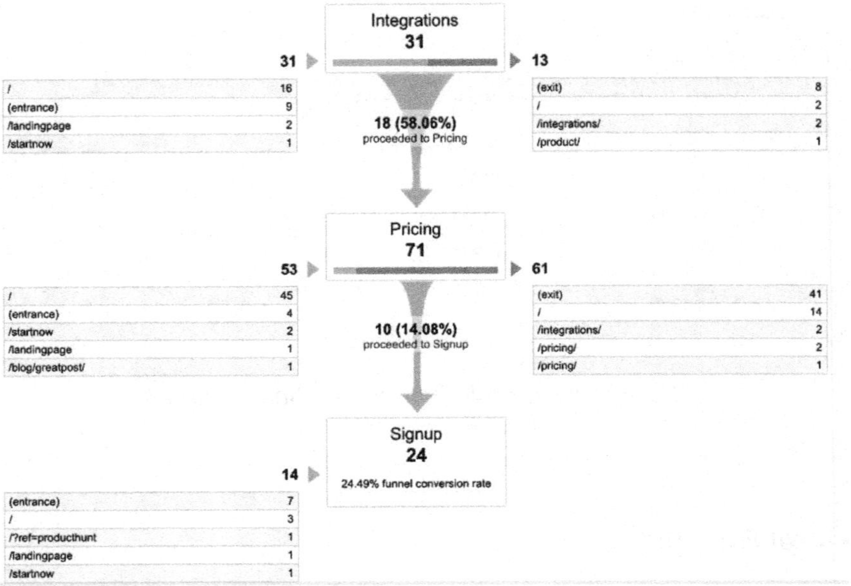

In this funnel, we can see that most people go straight to the Pricing page and that 14.08% continue to Signup.

The *Goal Flow* looks like this:

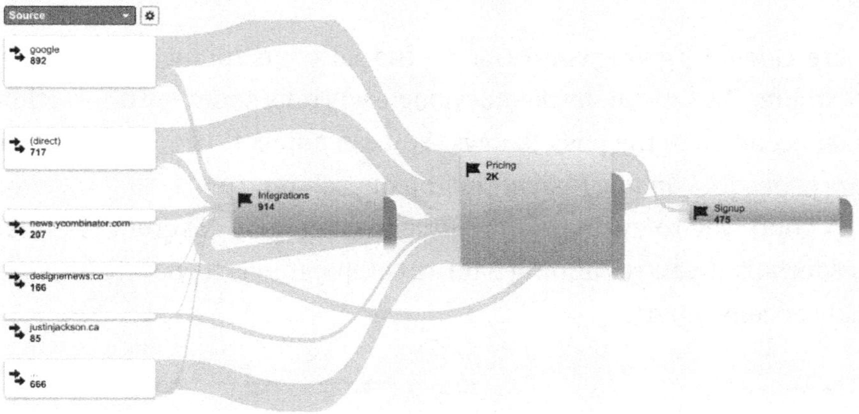

Google's Goal Flow highlights how traffic moves through your funnel

View the steps it takes to achieve a goal

People typically don't just type your website into their browser, add your product to the shopping cart, and buy. There are usually multiple touch points along the way. Most e-commerce reports only give credit to whatever the last referral was.

To see how each channel contributes to your overall conversions, go to *Goals >> Multi-Channel Funnels.*

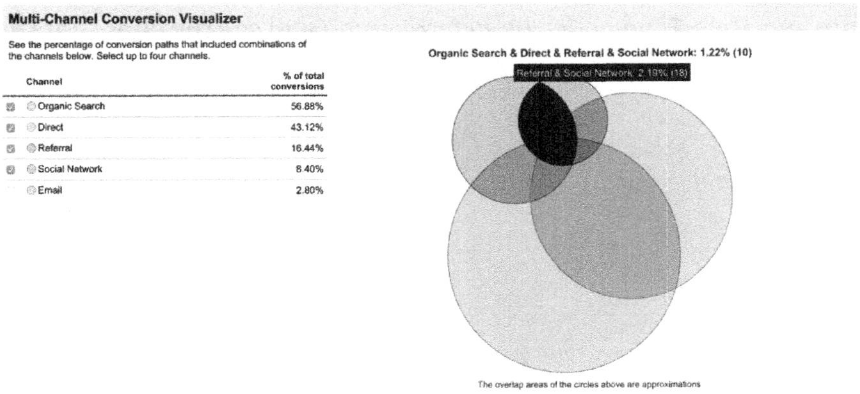

Multi-Channel Conversion Visualizer

Here, Google is giving you an idea of the path a visitor takes to become a customer. Be careful: by default Google will only show you interactions that occurred in the past 30 days. You can adjust this up to 90 days in the *Lookback Window* field at the top of each report.

A good way to evaluate the monetary value of different channels (especially if you're running paid ad campaigns) is to view the *Assisted Conversions* report.

	MCF Channel Grouping	Assisted Conversions ↓	Assisted Conversion Value	Last Click or Direct Conversions	Last Click or Direct Conversion Value	Assisted / Last Click or Direct Conversions
1.	Paid Search	80 (74.07%)	$5,808.00	92	$6,500.00	0.87
2.	Organic Search	13 (12.04%)	$809.00	4	$247.00	3.25
3.	Referral	10 (9.26%)	$791.00	3	$198.00	3.33
4.	Social Network	2 (1.85%)	—	2	$9.00	1.00

The Assisted Conversions report

In this example, we can see that *Paid Search* is driving the bulk of sales, and that leads from *Social Networks* are converting very little. This could be a signal to try something new with a channel that's not working or to double down on a channel that's converting well.

You can also click each of these channel groupings and drill down into specifics. If you click on *Referrals,* you will see the sites that sent you your best-converting traffic.

10

Using Mixpanel

Mixpanel is another analytics tool, similar to Google Analytics. However, it excels in a few areas, notably with real-time tracking, funnels, and the way it reports on events.

If you've followed my advice and linked to your Segment account to Mixpanel, you should see this when you log in:

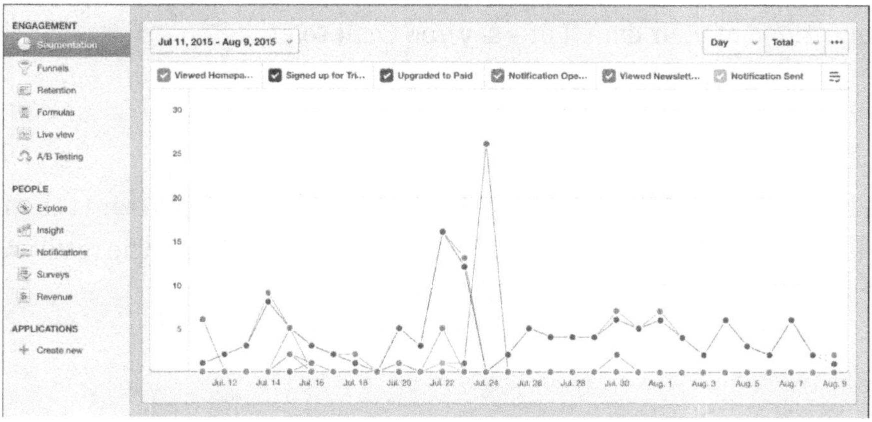

Mixpanel's Segmentation report

The event data you identified when setting up Segment is already populated here in Mixpanel.

You'll notice that Mixpanel offers many reports. In this chapter we'll be covering:

- Segmentation
- Funnels
- Explore
- Insight
- Notifications

Segmentation

As a default, Segmentation will show you a chart of your top 12 events with the most volume. It will give you a high-level view of how people are using your website and app, and help you observe trends. For example: in the image above, there was a spike in people who upgraded on July 24.

However, the real power with Segmentation is the ability to ask questions of your data. Let's say you want to know:

> *Where do most of our paying customers come from?*

First, you would choose your *New Paying Customer* event from the top drop-down. Then, you would segment by *Referral Source*. The resulting chart would look something like this:

Segmentation allows you to ask your data questions

From this chart, we could infer that Facebook Ads are driving more conversions than other sources of traffic lately. I can also segment by additional dimensions (countries, plan type, gender). As with anything, the more data events you collect, the better you can understand your customers.

Funnels

We introduced the idea of funnels in the Google Analytics chapter. What I like about Mixpanel's funnels is they focus on user *actions*, as opposed to page views. They're also much easier to slice up on the fly.

To create your first funnel in Mixpanel, click *Funnels* in the side navigation, and then click *Build a Funnel.*

The interface is quite a bit easier to grok than Google's. You enter, in succession, the events you'd like to track:

Building a funnel in Mixpanel

Before you click *Save*, take a look in the bottom right-hand corner. There's a little time clock icon there with the default *30 days to convert* selected. If you click that icon, you'll get options that look like this:

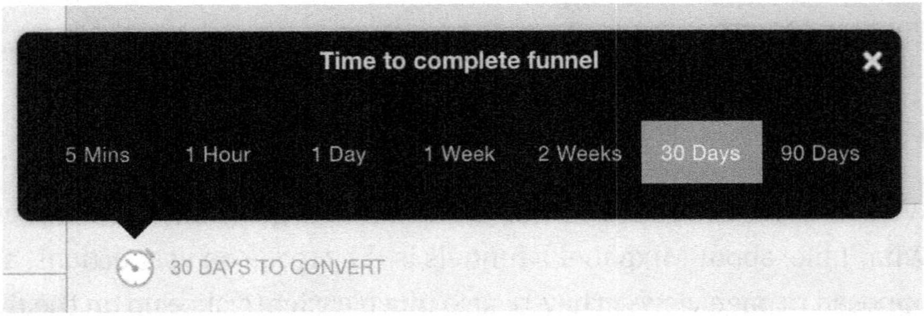

Find this option before you save your funnel

Mixpanel is asking you, "How much time does it take to complete this funnel?" Your options are 5 minutes, 1 hour, 1 day, 1 week, 2 weeks, 30 days, and 90 days. If you have a SaaS business with a 30-day free trial, you will select *30 days*. However, if you offer a 3-month trial, you'll want to select *90 days*. Conversely, if you're selling an eBook that has a 7-day free email course leading into it, you might choose *1 week*.

Once you click *Save*, you'll see your funnel visualized like this:

A saved funnel

Each step in the funnel is represented by a bar graph. You can click each bar and further segment the data. For example, you could segment *Created Account* by country. In between each bar is the conversion rate (8.8% and 76.33% respectively above). You can also drill into this data by clicking on the conversion rate and seeing a trend line over time.

Explore

Under the *People* heading in the side navigation, you'll find *Explore*. This is my favorite part of Mixpanel, especially if you're just starting to get new users or customers.

At first glance, *Explore* is just a list of people who have signed up on your website.

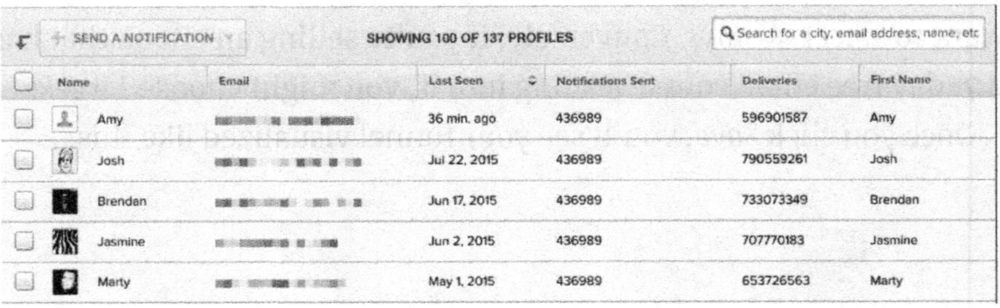

Explore provides you with a list of users

However, clicking on any of these profiles will reveal something amazing: the journey that person took to becoming a customer. If *Segmentation* and *Funnels* are the macro views, *Explore* and, specifically, *User Profile* is the micro view.

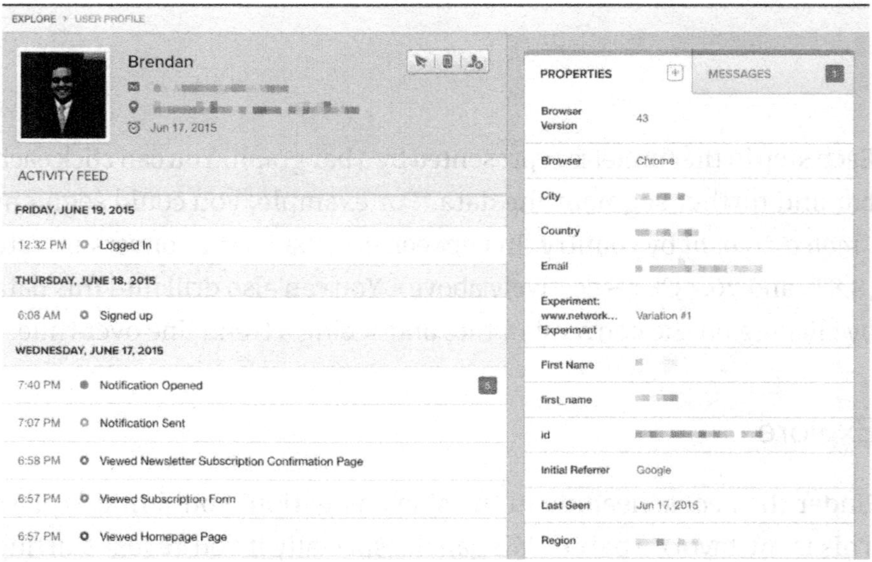

You can see your customer's journey in User Profile

In this screenshot, we see that Brendan came to our homepage from a Google search on a Wednesday night. From there he subscribed to the waiting list email. We sent him a sign-up link that night by email, but he waited until the following day to sign up. Then he waited until Friday (perhaps on his lunch break) to log in for the first time.

> ***Bonus tip:*** *I like to take these user profiles and turn them into full customer journeys by looking at the contact's Twitter, LinkedIn, and other profile information and overlaying any significant events that occurred on top. Sometimes you'll find that a tweet, or email to customer support, preceded the sign-up event.*

If I want more customers like Brendan, digging into the details of how he became a customer can be helpful. I might learn that many of my valuable customers interacted with my blog three times before they clicked "Sign up." If I check who else they follow on Twitter or are connected to on LinkedIn, I might discover that many of these customers are connected with each other.

These clues are especially helpful early on when you don't have very many customers. Finding out why one person signed up might help you find other people like them.

Insight

Mixpanel's Insight section allows you to create interactive trend lines with your data. If you wanted to segment "Signups by Plan" your graph would look something like this:

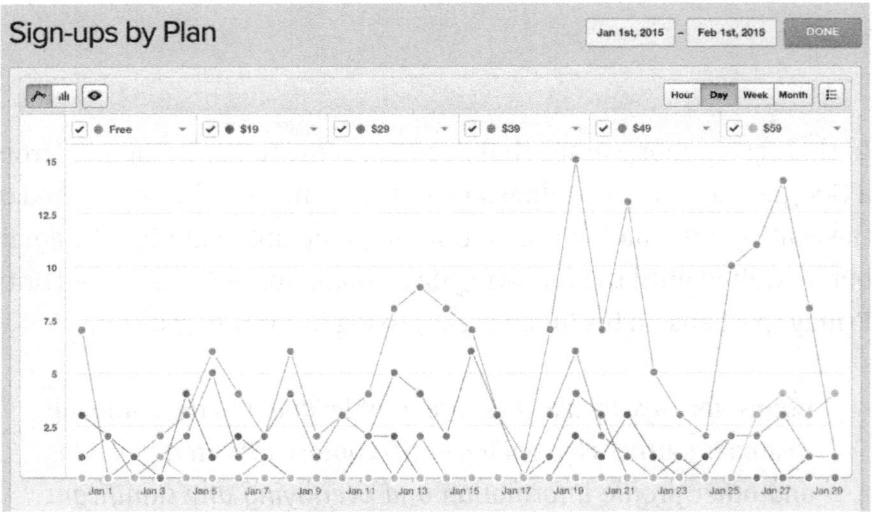

A sample Insight graph

Once you've generated the graph by its segment, you can further filter by *Customers that match all of / any* different properties. For example, in the report above we may want to filter by *Timezone* to see if higher priced sign-ups are coming from a certain area.

How to use this data

Look for spikes, and try to cross-reference those with particular marketing campaigns you might be running. Was there a spike in new users on January 19 because your site got some media attention?

Also, observe trends: are there certain plans or tiers that are becoming less popular?

The more data you collect on customers, the more insights you'll be able to generate. Some products will include a brief survey when users sign up that includes demographic information like *Industry*, *Job Title*, and *Company Size*.

Any user information you collect can be used as a filter

These properties will allow you to ask deeper questions of your data. Questions like:

- How many of our signups came from companies with 1–10 employees?
- How many of our account holders are Product Managers?
- Are we still getting many government signups?

When you discover a significant trend, it gives you a new hypothesis to test. For example: if you discover that Product Managers are a significant source of income, you could try targeting that group with Facebooks Ads.

Notifications

In this book, I've spoken quite a bit about the power of email in marketing. I'd be remiss if I didn't mention Mixpanel's built in notification feature. You can send a variety of message types: email, SMS, push notification, webhooks, and in-app message.

Using the same property filters available elsewhere, you can trigger automatic emails to specific individuals, depending on where they are in the marketing funnel. For example, you might want to send users an email five days after they sign up to see how their trial is going:

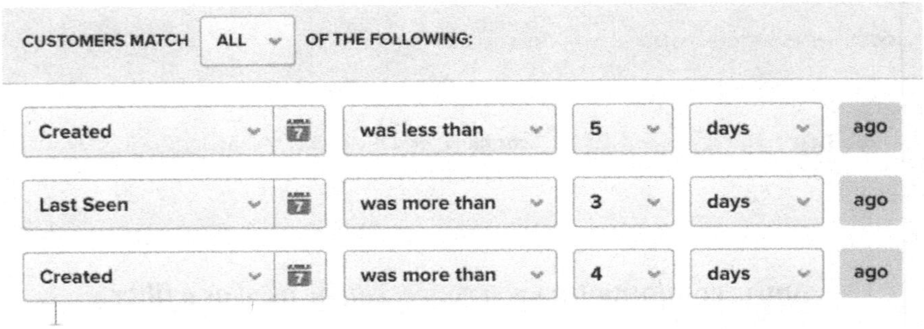

Target specific users by using criteria

You might also include a link that allows users to upgrade to a paying account.

What's great about Mixpanel's notifications is you can view them in your funnels, to see how they affect your conversion and upgrade rates:

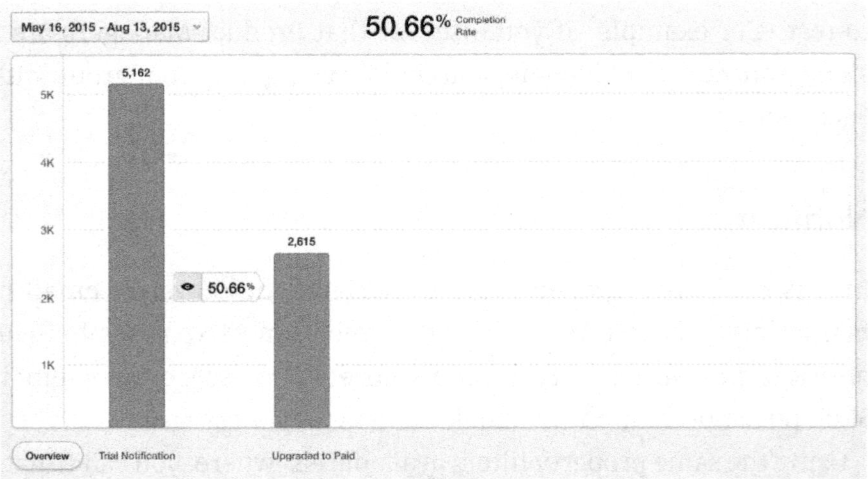

See how notifications affect your funnels

Here are other options with *Notifications:*

- **A/B tests:** create different versions of your message, and see which variant converts better.
- **Mail merge:** insert variables in your message (first name, trial remaining, product purchased) and Mixpanel will dynamically fill them as they are sent.
- **Scheduling:** you can trigger emails to be sent immediately, or you can schedule them to be sent at a particular of day.
- **In-app notifications:** just like email, you can send in-app notifications for both mobile and web applications. Want to trigger a pop-up for users who haven't upgraded to your paid version? This is an excellent way to do that.

More resources

We've just scratched the surface of what's possible with Mixpanel. For further learning I recommend:

- mixpanel.com/blog/ - Mixpanel consistently posts new usage examples on their blog.

mixpanel.com/learn/ - You'll find Mixpanel's basic video tutorials here.

III

Before You Launch

11

Two marketing channels to focus on

There are numerous marketing channels you can use:

- **Word of mouth:** people telling other people about what you're building
- **Ads:** Facebook Ads, Adwords, LinkedIn ads, etc.
- **Partnerships:** finding other companies that have a similar audience to you, and cross-promoting
- **Events:** throwing a party, hosting a conference
- **Traditional lead-gen and sales:** purchasing lists, cold-calls
- **SEO:** finding relevant keywords, and writing good content that matches those keywords
- **Content marketing:** blogging, info graphics, viral videos, good landing pages
- **Email marketing:** building an interest-based list, sending weekly newsletters

I've tried all of these. I've tried them with SaaS businesses and digital products (like eBooks, and downloadable software). For me, and everyone I know, **content marketing** + **email marketing** is the clear winner.

> *"If your goal is to build a business and make sales, and you could only pick one channel, it'd be tough not to choose email. It's a*

> *push notification as opposed to a pull notification. You get to send them a message to their 'sacred space': their inbox."*
> *- Corbett Barr, Fizzle*

Before you launch (and after) I'm going to recommend that you focus primarily on content marketing and email. Together, they'll give you all the ammo you'll need to create buzz about your product, positive word of mouth, and ultimately, more sales.

Why email works

Nobody likes getting spam. As technical people, we're particularly averse to it.

However, email is still the internet's best marketing channel.

> *"My email list is my most valuable asset."*
> *- Nathan Barry*

Why, in the age of social media, is email still your most effective tool for reaching customers?

Email is for grownups

While teenagers might prefer texting on mobile apps like YikYak and Snapchat, email is still the dominant messaging medium for adults. Think about it: each step towards adulthood brings with it an increase in email usage. When you go to college, you receive a school email address. When you get a job, you get a corporate email address.

So while only 11% of teens use email on a daily basis[13], 91% of adults check it daily[14], and 470 million of the world's email accounts are

---

13 Pew Internet, 2010

14 ExactTarget, Mobile Behavior Report, 2014

corporate.[15]

> *"The inbox is where work happens. People run their businesses off email. It's read and acted on, or ignored."*
> *- Brennan Dunn*

When you have a product, you want to target people with money. Adults with email addresses (especially corporate email addresses) are employed or own their own business. Most people's problem solving occurs in their inbox. That's where you want to be.

Email is a daily habit

In 2013, Lifehacker asked its readers this question: *What's the first thing you check each morning?*

The responses were as follows:

- Email: 44.77%
- Social networks: 17.23%
- News: 8.77%
- Favorite website: 8.42%
- RSS feeds: 8.32%
- To-do list or calendar: 3.52%
- Other: 8.97%

When people wake up, they roll over and reach for their cell phone. The first thing most of them are checking is email.

Email has more permanence

Posting a link on Twitter is like dropping a paper boat in a rushing river. Your tweet is quickly lost in people's feeds.

---

[15] Pingdom, 2010

An email, however, will sit in a recipient's inbox until they act on it. Confirmed open rates for email trend between 25% and 50%. A tweet will normally be seen by only 10% of your followers.[16]

Email captures website traffic

A normal website visitor listens to your pitch once. If they leave, they're gone forever. There's no way of following up, and there's no way of presenting your product's value differently. You need a way of capturing those drive-by visitors. One way is doing retargeting ads, which we'll discuss later. The best way to nurture leads from "interested" to "purchased" is with email.

Email converts to more sales

I recently ran a sales campaign that used three main channels: email, Twitter, and my website. Here are the sales breakdowns:

- **Email:** 263 sales (12% conversion from 2,192 visitors)
- **My website:** 37 sales (6% conversion 616 visitors)
- **Twitter:** 8 sales (1% conversion from 800 visitors)

Of course, your conversion rates will depend on your audience and your product. But across all markets, email consistently outperforms other channels. In a 2014 survey, 57% of marketing managers said that email was their top lead generation channel.[17]

Tactics to grow your list

Now that we've covered the *why* in the next chapters will dig into the *how*. This includes specific tactics for writing great content that

[16] linkedin.com/pulse/20140711200612-7775134-new-twitter-analytics-reveal-10-organic-reach

[17] DialogTech, 2014 Marketing Measurement Survey Report

attracts new subscribers to your mailing list.

12

The landing page cheat sheet

A landing page is single page website with one goal: to get people to convert. Your goal might be to get more email signups. It might be to have more people sign-up for a trial. Best of all, it might be to convince people to *buy your product.*

During the marketing process, you'll likely build many of these sites. Here's a framework for building effective, high converting, landing pages:

What do you want to achieve?

First, identify what you want your landing page to achieve. For example, in the months leading up to your launch, your primary goal is to build an email list. After you launch, your main goal will be to get people to buy your product.

To get started, write out a statement like this:

> *The main point of this landing page is to help (this person) understand (this promise). The main goal is to have them (perform this action).*

Here's an example from the company, *Send With Us.* Their target audience is *marketers.* A marketer's biggest challenge is they can't get anything done without the help of a developer.

sendwithus.com/marketers

They might write their main objective like this:

- **Target audience:** marketers.
- **Main point:** *Send With Us* helps marketers edit transactional emails without a developer's help.
- **Main promise:** marketers will get more engagement and revenue.

In this case, the page's objective is to have visitors sign up for a trial.

Sections of a landing page

Headline + Sub-headline

The first thing people read is your main headline. Don't waste it! It's your way to hook people's interest. Ask these questions while forming your headline and sub-headline:

1. Who is this for?
2. What's their dream of a better life?
3. What obstacle stands in their way?

4. How do you help them overcome that obstacle?

Use "you" language

The headline is not the place to introduce yourself. Instead, address your audience directly by using (or implying) the word "you."

Here are a few examples of *bad* "we" focused headlines:

- "Corporate gifting by Sesame."[18]
- "We make interfaces."[19]
- "Lita Healthcare Group Limited is a diversified healthcare company which markets and distributes products to the hospital and retail healthcare environment."

On the flip-side, here are some *good* audience-focused headlines:

- "Accounting made for you, the non-accountant."[20]
- "You don't need to be an engineer. Build your startup by pointing and clicking."[21]
- "Guaranteed to increase your organic search traffic."[22]

Use verbs

Improve your headlines by using a strong *verb*. Without a primary *action*, headlines feel like generic descriptions:

- "Dead simple time tracking."[23]

---

[18] sesamegifts.com

[19] metalab.co

[20] freshbooks.com

[21] bubble.is

[22] hittail.com

[23] ding.io

- "Real-time customer activity all in one place."[24]
- "Meet the world's first visual CMS."[25]

Here are headlines that make good use of verbs:

- "Create professional client proposals in minutes."[26]
- "Record bugs easily."[27]
- "Send with confidence. Build, test, and monitor your emails with Litmus."[28]

Landing page body

Now we get to the meat of the page. Follow this checklist while crafting your content for the body:

- **Put a visual near the top.** An image or a video can help people imagine themselves using the product. Images that create an emotional response are particularly helpful.
- **List the benefits:** in what ways does your product help your audience?
- **Show social proof.** Are notable people using it? What trusted news sources have written about it?
- **Describe some (not all) of your features.** Remember to describe the product itself! List a few features, and describe what makes them unique.
- **Call to action:** what is the conversion event for your page? If it's to get people signed up for your list, feature your sign-up form prominently. If it's to get people to buy, focus on your pricing tiers

---

[24] woopra.com

[25] webflow.com

[26] bidsketch.com

[27] testfire.io

[28] litmus.com

and "Buy Now" buttons.

Footer

Keep the footer simple. You don't want to give people too many reasons to click on a link and leave the landing page. Start with three links and/or short content sections:

1. **About:** who is behind this project?
2. **Blog:** link to your blog.
3. **Contact:** provide a way for people to contact you to ask questions.

Focus on the words

Jason Fried, the founder of Basecamp, has a great metaphor for building landing pages:

> *I've got to start with the words; the story has to be right. You can launch with just words.*

Before you work on the design, images, and formatting, **focus on the words.** Here is Jason's template for writing landing pages:

> ***What***
> *What feature/product are we talking about?*
>
> ***Why***
> *Why does the audience care?*
>
> ***The pitch***
> *A short paragraph that sells the "What" to the audience.*

How it works

A description of how the feature works

Case study: Bidsketch

Here is the Bidsketch landing page. Pay particular attention to how they leverage social proof.

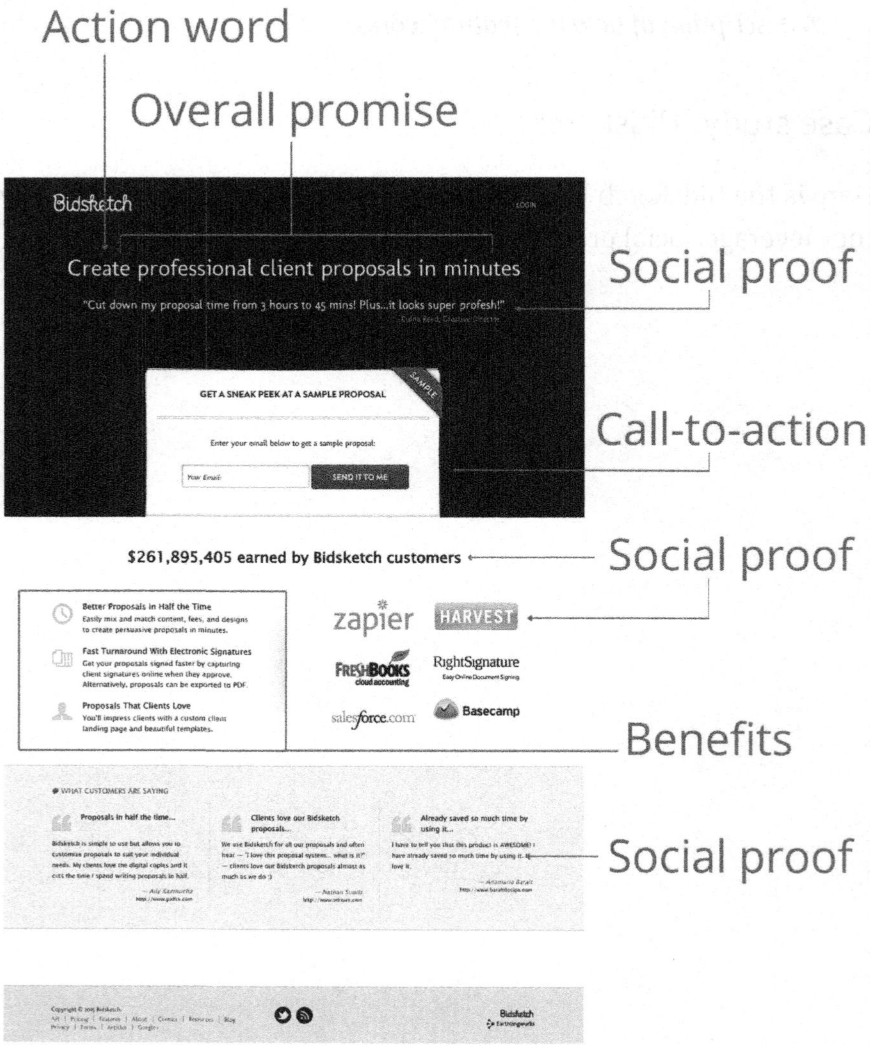

bidsketch.com

Reuben, the founder of Bidsketch, is emphasizing two promises to business owners:

1. **Bidsketch will save you time:** "Create professional client propos-

als in minutes."

2. **Bidsketch will make you money:** "$261,895,405 earned by Bidsketch customers."

The page is minimal, lightweight, and focused on one goal: getting people to sign up for a sample template.

For more landing page inspiration, you can visit www.landingfolio.com.

13

How to write blog posts that get noticed

Growing an audience and launching a product is more than just following a system. The magic glue that makes it work is your online reputation. If you want to sell something to a group of people, you need to earn their trust. How do you gain their trust? You teach them.

> *"If you want to be useful, you can always start now. It will be a humble prototype of your grand vision, but you'll be in the game. Start by teaching someone this week. Starting small puts 100% of your energy into solving real problems for real people."*
> *- Derek Sivers,*

Your blog should be a sneak peek into the value your product provides. To ensure you get maximum traction, you'll want to follow three steps:

1. Research your audience.
2. Write unique content that your audience wants to read.
3. Amplify your content to reach new people.

Research first

Writing good blog posts requires research.

Do research in communities where your target market hangs out.

Here are some examples:

- Designers: Designer News
- Retail store owners: TalesFromRetail
- Hardcore developers: Lobsters
- Marketers: Inbound.org or GrowthHackers

While you're there, look for opportunities where you can help. What pain points come up repeatedly? These pain points can become topics for your blog.

Write good stuff

Everyone's writing blog posts: how can you make yours stand out? Your biggest asset is what you know about your audience. Talk about the issues they care about.

> *It's not about you; it's about them. Every post should focus on the needs of your audience.*

Here are some ideas for making your blog posts stand out:

- **Focus on one point per post.** It's easy to veer into a tangent when writing. Stay focused on one idea, and communicate that idea as efficiently as possible.
- **Use diagrams, illustrations, cartoons.** My most shared blog posts all have this element in common. Illustrations are often shared as the featured image in tweets and Facebook posts. Because of this, I'll often have illustrations done professionally.
- **Put something *surprising* in your post.** We make fun of Buzzfeed headlines like, "This grandma ordered grilled cheese on the internet; you won't believe what happened next!" They're tapping into human nature. We're all attracted to stories that shock us or have a bombshell revelation at the end. These are also the stories we're most likely to *share*.

- **Jump on trends and current events.** Is everyone talking about it? It can be difficult to rise above the noise when discussing current trends (like reviews on the latest Apple gadget). However, if you have a unique point of view that hasn't been covered, your message has a greater chance of being amplified.
- **Make people laugh**. A good sense of humor is a tremendous asset. So much of online content is banal. Being funny is a great way to get noticed.
- **Share your process.** People like to hear the behind-the-scenes tales of how you're building your product. Show them some code! Talk about a technical challenge and how you overcame it.
- **Teach them something new.** Did you just figure out how to build a Slack integration? Teach other people to do it, too! Just recorded your first screencast? Write up a tutorial, and publish it on your blog.

Remember, growing your audience is more than just following a system. To get people's attention, create content that is interesting, unique and trustworthy.

Amplify your content

Blog posts, videos, and podcasts are valuable marketing tools. You can use them to reach new prospects, and expand your audience.

But *creating* content isn't enough. Amplification is about taking what you've created and distributing it through other people's networks. There are three types of amplifiers you should focus on:

1. **Individual influencers:** these are individuals who have built an audience in the market you're targeting. These could be popular bloggers, podcasters, entrepreneurs, journalists, or people with a big following on Twitter.
2. **Online networks:** these are community sites, forums, news sites, aggregators, Facebook groups, and anywhere else where people

in your target market congregate.

3. **Your network:** this is your email list and the people who follow you on social media.

Build relationships with influencers carefully! Alex Turnball, of Groovehq.com, did a great job of this when he sent me this email (from his personal Gmail address):

> *Hey Justin,*
>
> *I know you probably get a ton of emails from startups looking for your expertise, so I'll keep this really short. I think you might find it interesting...*
>
> *I'm launching a new series on my blog this week hoping to take an honest look at the long, tough haul from idea to a successful company. Specifically, I'm tracking the ups and downs of going from zero users (where we were) to $28k in monthly revenue (where we are) to $100k/month, and beyond.*
>
> *Would love to share it with you if you're interested. Do you mind if I send you a link?*
>
> *Thanks,*
> *Alex*

He sent similar emails to other influencers in his space (people like Gary Vaynerchuk, Dan Martell, and Rob Walling). He found that 83% of the people he emailed responded positively.

Why? He wasn't forceful. Notice he doesn't even include a link to the post in his email. He only asks if I want to see it. Also, his proposal is unique and appeals directly to the people he's emailing. The idea of Alex sharing his revenue and growth tactics is compelling for any software entrepreneur.

The game plan

Once you have a group of influencers ready to share your content, follow this checklist:

1. Give influencers, and your network, a sneak peek at your blog post and ask for feedback.
2. Revise your post based on their feedback.
3. Set a "launch date" for your post.
4. Let the influencers and your list know when you're going to publish and how they can help.
5. Publish your post!
6. Share your post on online networks (Reddit, Hacker News).
7. Email influencers and ask them to share and provide traction on community sites. Now that they've offered their opinion, they have a vested interest in its success.
8. Respond to those who engage with your content (in comments, and on social media).
9. Look for opportunities to expand the discussion or cross-post to new networks.
10. Thank everyone who shares it!

Having a plan will give your content a better chance of gaining traction. Instead of "publish, wait and see" you're working proactively.

> *There's this fallacy that good content always gets discovered, but the truth is that content needs distribution in to be seen.*

Case study

I've used this approach dozens of time to drive traffic to a blog post.

A recent example is a blog post I wrote for Sprintly, called *Your*

Developers Aren't Slow.[29]

Reading that headline, you can almost predict that this blog post is going to hit a nerve.

Following the checklist above, that blog post generated over 100,000 page views that month. The article has over 6,000 shares on social media (their competitor's best post has 1,500 shares). The post also increased organic email leads by 32% within 48 hours. Best of all, the post resulted in new sign ups for Sprintly:

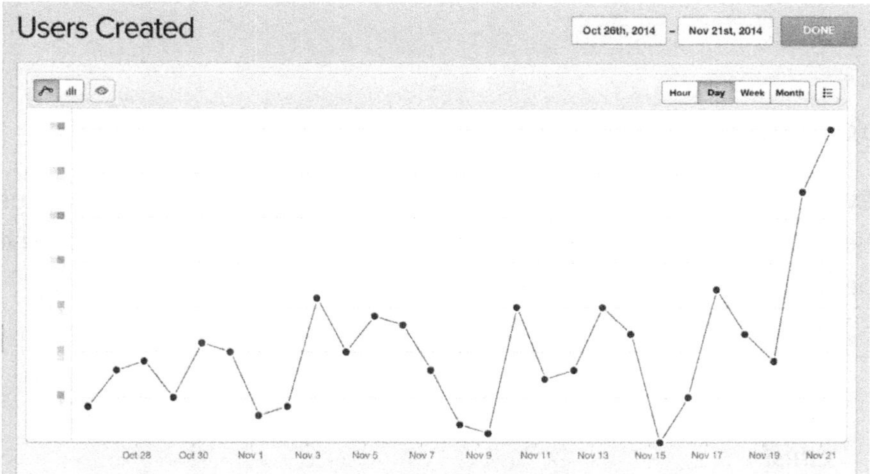

New trials increased 3x

These results show that leveraging the right channels can help your content gain significantly more traction.

[29] *https://sprint.ly/blog/your-developers-arent-slow/*

14

How to build an email list

Your subscription form

Every blog post and landing page you create should have a call to action. Before you launch your product, your primary CTA will be to have people *subscribe to your email list.*

Your sign-up form is a way of saying:

> *Did you find this content helpful? Let me send you more stuff like this!*

Where should you put your subscription form?

The positioning of your subscription form is important. There are many approaches; test each option to see if one converts better for you.

Inline

Traditionally, email forms were put in the right-hand sidebar at the top. Here's the challenge: when the visitor is finished reading, they're at the bottom of the page (and unlikely to scroll back up).

Nowadays, it's much more common to place the subscription form inline, in the content block. This could be at the top of the blog post, in the middle, or at the end.

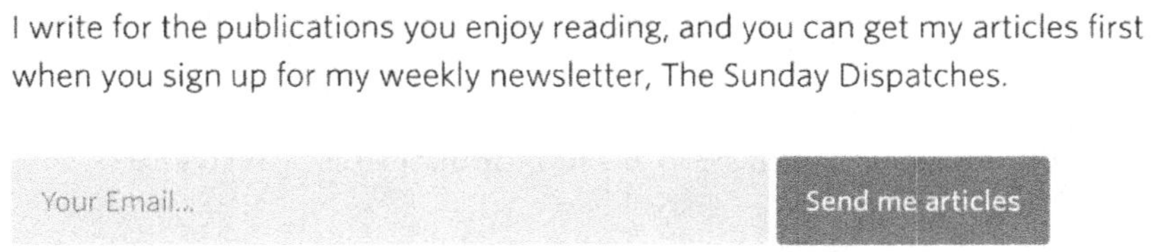

Paul Jarvis puts his subscription form at the end of each post.

Modal

Another option is to show a pop-up modal.

While the reader scrolls, you can have some JavaScript fire to show a pop-up. These can be shown on the side of the page (so as not to interfere with reading) or they can cover the content (so they can't be missed). Another option is to display the modal after a certain amount of time has passed. While some people find these annoying, they can result in high opt-ins.

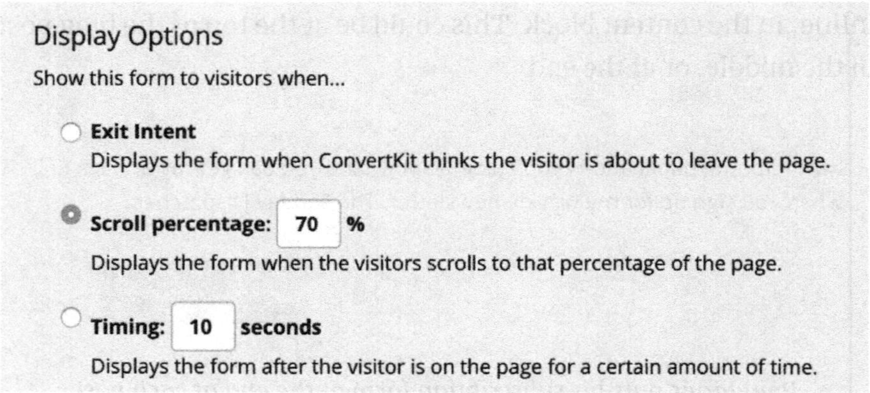

ConvertKit allows you to choose how you'd like the modal to fire

The final option is to show the pop-up during "exit intent." When the reader finishes the article and moves their cursor to close the tab, you fire some JavaScript that shows a pop-up.

This can be effective because the reader is already finished viewing the page and allows you to catch them before they leave. Ouibounce is an open source library (available on GitHub) for creating this type of modal.[30]

Send email regularly

How many times have you received an email that says, "We've launched!" but you can't remember who the company is, what they're building, or why you signed up?

Once someone signs up, you need to keep in regular contact with them. This serves three purposes:

1. Helps your subscribers remember who you are, and what you're building.

---

30 github.com/carlsednaoui/ouibounce

2. Provides immediate value.
3. Builds anticipation for your launch.

The best way to provide value is to share what you're learning as you make your product. Did you write a JavaScript library that's been helpful? Share it with your list!

15

Set a price

Setting a price for your product can be the most difficult part of the marketing process. Here are three techniques to get you started.

Price based on value

One way to sell your product is to show customers how it can **make them money, save them money, or save them time**. You're not selling an ebook, a web application, or a certain feature: you're selling an outcome.

Choose your price by extrapolating what someone would pay you to help them achieve their goal.

One method of doing this *is the 10x value proposition*: provide the same value as the current solution but for 10x less. For example, instead of going to a $2,000 conference, a customer could buy your $200 online workshop.

Conference vs online workshop	Cost
Conference	$2,000
Online workshop	$200
Savings	$1,800

Price based on LTV

Lifetime value (LTV) - cost per acquisition (CPA) = profit

To make a profit, you'll need to earn more money per customer than it costs to acquire that user.

For a single use product, the lifetime value of that user will usually be the price they paid. So, if a customer buys a book from you for $20, then that customer is worth $20.

The calculation is different for products with recurring revenue. Here, you multiply the monthly price ($20) by the number of months a typical customer pays. If the average user pays for 12 months, your LTV would be 12 x $20 = $240.

Once you know customer LTV, subtract the amount it cost you to acquire that customer (CPA). So, if you spent $2,000 marketing your new online workshop, and 16 people bought, your CPA was $125. If you'd set a price of $200 per attendee, your profit per customer would be $75 (or $1,200 total).

Price using tiers

Gumroad[31] is an online marketplace for makers. They've done a considerable amount of research on the effect of pricing on revenue. One result: products with pricing tiers generated five times more revenue than those without.

> *"Your audience is a spectrum. It's everyone from people who just found out about you, all the way up to super fans. If you're only releasing products at one price point, you're missing a huge part of that spectrum. The top 1–2% of your audience would be willing to buy [an expensive] package if you made it available to them."*
> *- Ryan Delk, Gumroad*

The tiers that Ryan recommends are as follows:

- **Low tier:** this is your base product. If you're selling a SaaS, this is likely your $29 tier.
- **Middle tier:** this should be 2.2–2.5x your lowest tier.
- **High tier:** this level is priced at 5x your lowest tier and offers the most value. It should contain all your features.

---

[31] gumroad.com

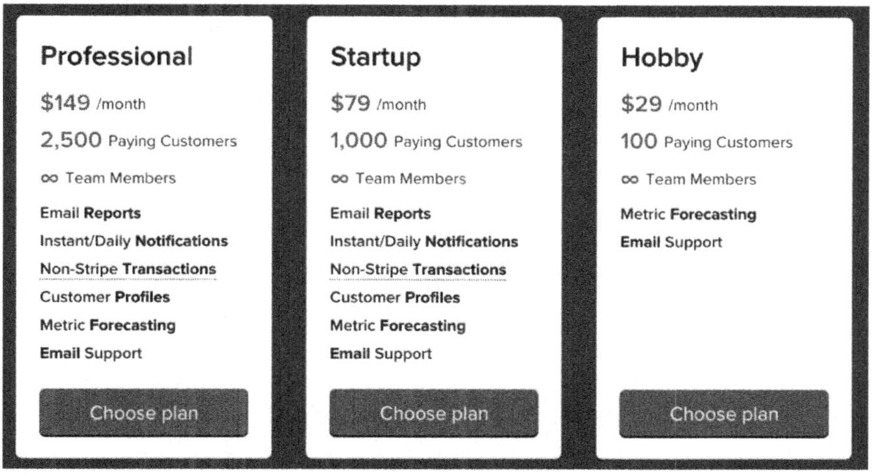

Baremetrics' pricing loosely follows the 1x, 2.5x, and 5x pricing strategy

There's anchoring psychology at work behind tiered pricing. The initial anchor price influences people's perception of value.[32]

> *"People make estimates by starting from an initial value."*
> *- Kahneman, Slovic and Tversky, Judgment Under Uncertainty*

Humans are wired to make comparisons. Provide them with only one price, and they'll go and comparison shop. Give them three prices, and they'll often make their decision at the moment. They use the context that's available instead of referencing an external source.

> *There's a certain group of people that will always buy the most expensive option. Duke University did a study where they offered students different groups of beers, all priced differently. 10% of*

---

[32] Orr, D. & Guthrie, C. (2005). "Anchoring, information, expertise, and negotiation: New insights from meta-analysis." Ohio St. J. Disp. Resol., 597, 21. SSRN 900152

students always bought the most expensive option.[33]

[33] Adding Asymmetrically Dominated Alternatives: Violations of Regularity and the Similarity Hyopthesis, Joel Huber; John W. Payne; Christopher Puto, The Journal of Consumer Research, June 1982

IV

Launching

16

How to build a street team

You can't do this alone.

To have a successful launch, you're going to need help from your network. Why? The more people you have talking about your product, the more reach you'll achieve.

Amplification

The web has a lot of noise. Because of that noise, most products don't break into the public consciousness, and therefore don't get discovered. This is especially evident when you look at Reddit, and what rises to the front page:[34]

[34] The reddit Front Page is Not a Meritocracy, toddwschneider.com/posts/the-reddit-front-page-is-not-a-meritocracy

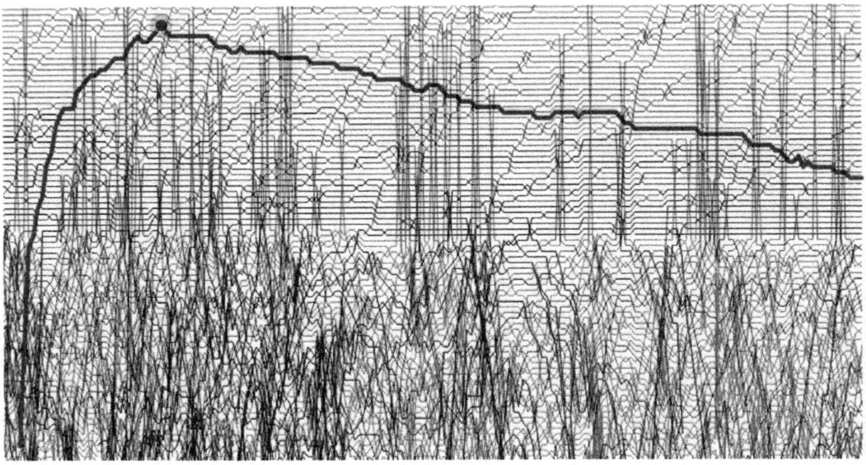

Reddit rankings over the course of a day

On Reddit, when a submission is ranked higher than 50, it climbs out of the noise below. Once it's ranked higher than 25, it's featured prominently on the front page.

To rise above the noise on the Internet, you'll need a critical mass of people who are sharing your product online. *Amplification* is a technique I use to create this momentum.

Essentially, *Amplification* has two parts:

- Create something worth sharing
- Engage with online networks that can help you share it

You'll need the help of both personal networks (your friends, the people you interact with on Twitter), and larger online networks (Reddit, Hackers News, and Product Hunt).

The first step is to engage with your network and build your street team.

Building a street team

A street team is a group of fans who want to help you with your launch. They'll generate word of mouth for your product by sharing it with *their* networks. How do you get people to assist you in this way? You ask them!

Make a list of everyone you know that might be interested in supporting your campaign.[35] Here's a list of people to consider:

- Early beta testers
- Enthusiastic email subscribers
- Your colleagues
- Your mentors
- People you've interacted with at events
- Members from groups and clubs you're a part of
- Friends and family

Once you have your list, reach out to each person and invite them individually. Here's an email template you can use:

> *Hi [name],*
>
> *As you know, I've been working on [my product]. The aim is to help [this type of person] with [this problem]. I'm about to launch on October 15th.*
> *I need your help.*
>
> *If this launch is going to be a success, I need to spread the word. I'm wondering if you could help me with two things:*
>
> *1. Today: share my current landing page with your friends. Here's is the link: http://yourlandingpage.com.*

[35] If you're looking for help on building your network, I go into specific tactics in this chapter: *Get more leads.*

> 2. *On launch day (October 15): submit my product to Product Hunt.*
>
> *Is this something you'd be willing to do?*
>
> *Cheers,*
> *[your name]*

Remember: these should be people you have a relationship with. Every once in a while, it's fine to ask your friends for a favor. Launching a new product is one of those times!

Gaining traction on online networks

Your product might lend itself to sites like Product Hunt, Hacker News, Reddit and Designer News. If so, it makes sense to have your street team help you gain traction on these sites.

First, let's talk about voting rings. Websites like Reddit want excellent content. What they don't want are groups of people (or bots) continuously upvoting each other en masse that bring low-quality submissions to the top. Each of these sites has algorithms to detect this type of behavior. The penalty is usually to ban the users involve (invalidate their accounts).

So, should you ask your friends to submit and upvote your submissions?

Personally, I think it's fine; especially if your content is helpful and applicable to that community. Truthfully, it's difficult to "game" these platforms. Through algorithms and moderation, they're usually able to weed out the bad stuff, even if a submission gets an initial boost. Ultimately, for something to stay at the top, it has to be high quality.

I feel like Product Hunt addresses this distinction well in their FAQ:[36]

---

[36] www.producthunt.com/faq#may-i-ask-people-to-upvote-for-my-product

> ***May I ask people to upvote for my product?*** *Please don't. People should upvote things they genuinely like or find interesting, not because they were peer pressured to do so. Feel free to spread the word and bring friends into the discussion, but asking or incentivizing people to upvote may trigger the algorithm to drop the product in the ranks or remove it from the front page entirely.*

I recommend following these guidelines:

1. Don't send people a direct link! Ask people to go directly to the site and search for the title of your submission manually.
2. You can have friends upvote your story, but do it prudently (and don't have the same friends vote every time). It's best if you can have different people from different countries vote on your story. This can be difficult to mobilize; I've found the best results in sending ten people an instant message right after submitting.
3. Announce it to your email list, and ask them to "share it, submit it and upvote it" if they like it. Having a large, diverse, audience will reduce the chance of being flagged by the voting ring detector.
4. Submitting your post to secondary networks first can be a good tactic. For example, if your story is relevant to designers, you could submit it to Designer News first. Often, a story makes it to the top of one network will be cross-posted to another.
5. Increase your chances of upvotes by posting at the right time (7 am - 12 pm EST) and having a great title.

People in your corner

Having a group who can help promote your product is a huge advantage in any market.

> *"Superfans will spread the word further, wider, and more passionately than any advertising could."*

- Jason Fried, David Heinemeier Hansson, Rework

Building a street team is hard work, and takes time, but pays high dividends. You won't be a lonely maker telling the world about your product; you'll have help.

17

Your launch plan

You've done all the hard work. You've picked a target market, you've discovered what people want, and you've built it. Now it's time to launch!

Launches can be scary. There's so much to do, and it's easy to get frazzled. This chapter will guide you through the process, so you can maintain your Zen without going off the rails.

Because every product is different, it's difficult to provide an exact launch timeline. What I've provided below is a general template. Please modify it to fit your product and your market!

Backward planning

Most people plan their launches sequentially. We're going to *work backward* from your launch day. Educators and industrialists have used reverse planning for years:[37]you start with the end objective and work backward, step by step until you get to the present day.

Launch day

Announce your launch by sending an email to your email list with a unique discount code that expires in 48 hours.

---

[37] Page 431, Foundations of Social Theory, By James S. Coleman

You should also mobilize your friends, early reviewers, and team to share the news on social media, and websites that your audience frequents.

Day before launch

Send an email to your list, reminding them that launch day is tomorrow. It should contain details like time, price, packages, the discount you'll offer, and answers to frequently asked questions.

Also, send an email to your friends, early reviewers, and team, prompting them to help you with tomorrow's launch. Coordinate who will help you post it to relevant sites: Product Hunt, Reddit, etc.[38]

Do a final test of everything:

- Is your payment processor working?
- Do you have analytics installed on your site?
- Is the pricing or sales page ready to go? Do all the links work? Is all the copy proofread?

7 days before launch

Write a blog post. The objective is to create anticipation for what you'll be launching in one week. Include a link to your landing page so that people can sign up for the waiting list.

Send an email to your list, getting them ready for the launch. Give them a tease: this could be a sample of the product, a screenshot, or a video demo.

Remind your "street team" about the launch date as well.

Your product itself should be 99% finished. At this point, you're just polishing it and doing final tests.

---

[38] For more information on this, see the *Research* chapter

1 month before launch

This is your final hustle. You're focused on your product; getting everything finished.

Remember to keep your email list and blog tuned into your progress. They want to hear the behind the scenes!

Tease out screenshots and early reviews through email and social media.

2 months before launch

Steady progress on your product. At this point, you should have something to show your beta list.

Send an email to your beta list and get people using your app. Watch them using the product in-person. Listen carefully to their first impressions. Take notes! Use this research to make your final product updates.

3 months before launch

Your first launch step should be to set up a landing page. This page should:

- State **who** your product is for.
- Show the primary **benefit** your product provides.
- Have a clear **call to action**: "Sign up for the waiting list," "Download a sample," "Join the beta!"

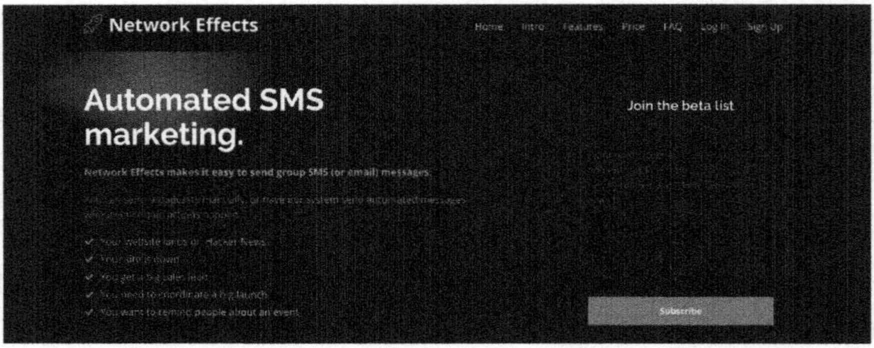

For software products, the call to action is often "Sign up for our beta!"

Your objective at this point is to get as many email sign-ups as you can. You can drive traffic to your landing page by:

- submitting to sites like betalist.com (you can find a full list at submit.co)
- sharing your landing page on social media and in your content
- guest posting on other blogs with a link to your landing page in your byline
- appearing on podcasts as a guest, and getting them to link to your landing page in the show notes

Get out your calendar

Now that you have an outline, it's time to get out your calendar. Working backward from your launch date, put each of these milestones in your calendars. If you're using Google Calendar (or something similar), get it to email you a reminder of each event. This will help keep you on track, especially if your head is in code!

The next chapter has a checklist you can use to keep track of your progress.

18

Your launch checklist

3 months before launch

- Set up a landing page for your product.
- Set up a mailing list for your product. Include subscription form on your landing page.
- Promote landing page on social media.
- Promote landing page by writing a guest post, appearing on a podcast, or creating your content.
- If applicable, submit to BetaList.com.

2 months before launch

- Share your progress with your mailing list.
- Get beta testers to start using an early version of the product.

1 month before launch

- Write a "behind the scenes" update for your blog and email list.
- Post teaser screenshots and early reviews to social media.

7 days before launch

- Write a blog post about the upcoming launch. Include a link to the waiting list.
- Send an email to the waiting list. Share sample, screenshot, or a video demo.
- Remind your street team about launch date as well, and outline how they can help.
- Do final tests on your product.
- Proofread landing page copy.

Day before launch

- Send an email to waiting list: should contain details like time, price, packages, the discount you'll offer.
- Send an email to your street team.
- Plan who will help you post it to relevant sites: Product Hunt, Reddit, etc.
- Ensure your payment processor is working.
- Test your site's analytics.
- Test links.
- Proofread announcement email and blog post.

Launch day

- Send an email to your email list with a special discount code.
- Send out an announcement on social media.
- Send a message to your street team with a pre-populated tweet. Ask them to share it with their friends!

Send out announcement to appropriate media sites.

V

After You Launch

19

How growth works

You've launched your product. What now?

Rob Walling once told me, "Making something people want isn't enough." It's true. Once you've launched a product, you need a steady stream of individuals lined up to buy it.

I get hundreds of emails from software developers who have built a product but can't find customers. Why is it so hard?

Markets are noisy

Most markets are filled with noise, and that's a problem.

Established players are already flooding existing channels with ads, articles, keywords, and social media posts. Your "new thing" is a drop of water in a rushing river: you're downstream before you know it, and nobody even saw you go.

Rising above that noise and *getting noticed* is hard.

Your audience isn't enough

You may already have built up an audience. Maybe you have a beta list, followers on Twitter, and people watching your blog. Awesome! That's an important first step.

However, if you want real market share, sending a tweet to a few hundred followers is not going to cut it.

> *"Having an audience is a nice kick starter. But then what? At some point, you have to learn other marketing skills, or you'll plateau."*
> *—Rob Walling,*

If you've built a high-quality product, you need to hook it up to the fastest engine possible: an engine that's able to connect you to the right markets.

Find a bigger, faster engine

That's what Josh Pigford, of Baremetrics, did when he hooked up with Buffer.

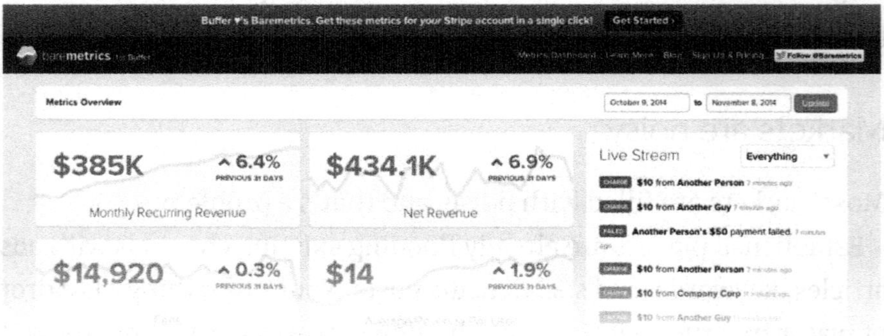

In 2014, Baremetrics and Buffer teamed up to offer open financial analytics

Josh has a product that provided SaaS applications with an automatic revenue dashboard. Buffer has built a huge audience through their content marketing efforts (they have over 1 million users and 240,000 followers on Twitter).

A big part of Buffer's marketing strategy is their transparency. They share everything: equity, salaries, pricing, fundraising, valuations.

Josh offered Buffer something new, a way to make their revenue metrics public: buffer.baremetrics.io. This provided great PR (and growth) for both parties.

In the seven days following the Buffer partnership, Josh increased the number of paying customers for Baremetrics by 27%.

Piggyback off another audience

Getting a piggyback is super helpful if you're a toddler and you're going on a big hike. On your parents' shoulders, you can cover way more distance than you could on your own.

The same goes for apps.

Here's an example: Hipstamatic and Instagram. Both offered a similar user experience: take a photo, and apply a filter. The difference was that Instagram hopped on Twitter's social graph. Users were able to sign up, instantly connect with the same people they followed on Twitter, and then tweet the photos they made on Instagram. Twitter hadn't introduced image sharing yet, so Instagram became the de facto service.

Parneet Gosal described this on PSFK:

> *On launch day, Twitter creator Jack Dorsey tweeted about it to his million+ followers. [But] having influential friends who know about your new service isn't enough. As co-founder Kevin Systrom disclosed at TechCrunch Disrupt NYC, Instagram's open social network and integration with other social sites have gone a long way in making it popular. [Users could] share their Instagram photos on Facebook, Twitter, and Flickr.*

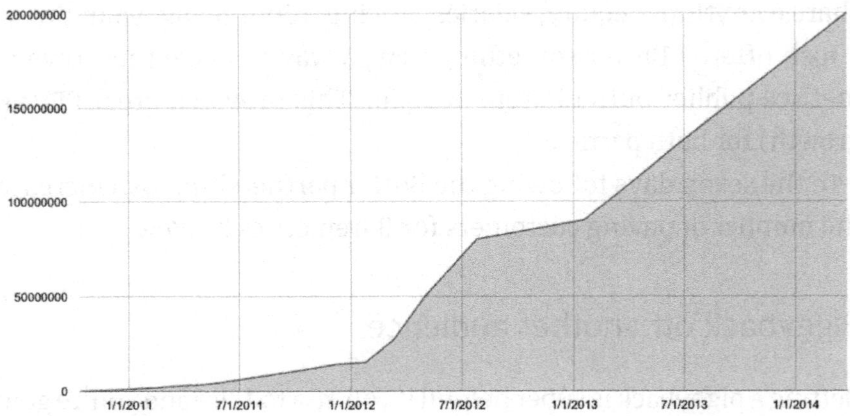

Instagram's user growth

Put simply, Instagram was able to grab users from Twitter. This is a big reason Twitter shut down API access to Instagram:

> *"We understand that there's great value associated with Twitter's follow graph data, and we can confirm that it is no longer available within Instagram."*
> *- Twitter spokesperson, Carolyn Penner, July 2012*

Piggybacking is using someone else's user graph. It's integrating with a platform where users already have social connections and are importing those links into your app.

Catch the big waves

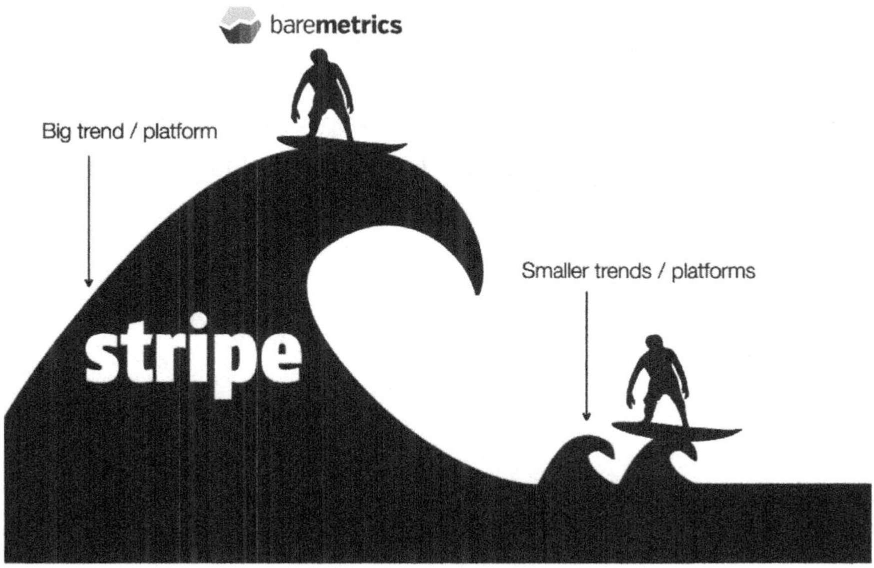

Baremetrics capitalized on an emerging trend: startups were increasingly using Stripe

Let's go back to my first example.

The other thing that helped Baremetrics was catching a big wave, in this case, the growing popularity of the Stripe platform.

A big wave is a significant trend or platform that comes rolling in like a giant swell. Stripe bubbled up in the developer community and eventually turned into a tsunami: it became the tool of choice for integrating payments into your web application.

Focusing specifically on Stripe allowed Josh to connect with the thousands of developers who were excited about that ecosystem. Yes, PayPal might have more users, but Stripe has momentum. You need the right timing to connect with a big wave; if you miss your window, the wave will be much smaller. Since Josh launched Baremetrics, many copycats have emerged, but they haven't had near the same traction.

How do you identify big waves? You stay vigilant. What are people talking about on Twitter? What are they searching for in Google? What are people talking about with their friends?

Many of us saw Slack, the group chat app, as it gained momentum. Look at this Google Trends report for the terms Slack, Hipchat, and Yammer:

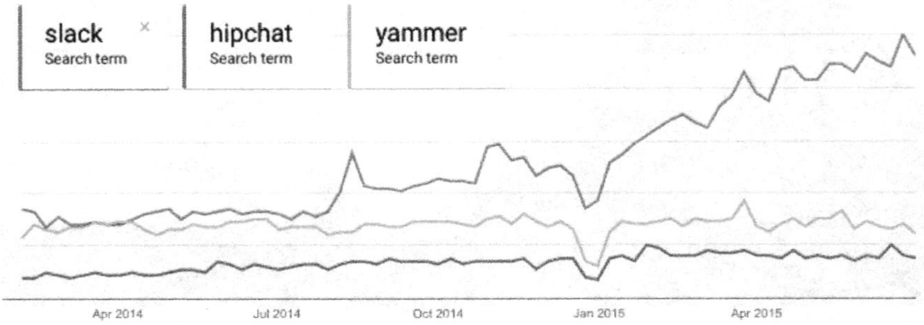

You can see interest in Slack, compared to other business-oriented chat apps, in Google Trends.

The key is to catch the wave while you can. Eventually, the surge will subside, and that channel will no longer be valuable. My friend Kyle Fox put it this way:

> *It is like a wave: you want to get on while it's peaking. But only expect to ride it so far. Then, paddle out and catch another.*

In summary

Find a speed train

These are the influencers in your industry. Look for the personalities (or brands) that have already built an audience. Hook your freight car to their engine: offer a partnership that benefits both parties.

Piggyback on an existing community

Integrate with platforms, especially those with a social graph. These integrations should allow users to easily import their existing connections from their address book or friends list.

Catch the big waves

Always be researching your niche. Be aware of trends that are building momentum. Take note of what people are talking about at industry events, in forums, and on social media. Observe and react to trends promptly! If you're too late, you might miss the wave.

Where to start

Not every tactic will work for you. In the following chapter, I'm going to give you a starting point: tactics you can use to acquire your first 100 customers.

20

SEO Basics

Search Engine Optimization is something that many product people ignore for far too long. But as you're going to see, there's nothing stronger than intent-based searches.

When someone has a struggle, question, or a problem, where do they go? They go to Google to look for an answer.

If your product is near the top of search results for those keywords you have a good chance of getting a customer. The person searching is intrinsically incentivized to solve their problem.

SEO is different from content marketing or posting on Product Hunt. On those sites, people are browsing recreationally. They're not looking for a solution.

In this chapter, I'll be using www.Roadmap.space, a product management tool, as an example. They help software companies generate public roadmaps.

Case study: Roadmap

My first step with Roadmap is to figure out how much organic search they're already getting. Specifically, which keywords are people using to find them?

The best place to find this information is in Google's Search Console (Webmaster Tools).

In the Search Console menu, go to:

1. Search Traffic
2. Search Analytics

Here, we're able to see how many clicks Roadmap has received for different queries on Google search.

Total clicks	Total impressions	Avg. CTR
2,170	84,000	2.58%

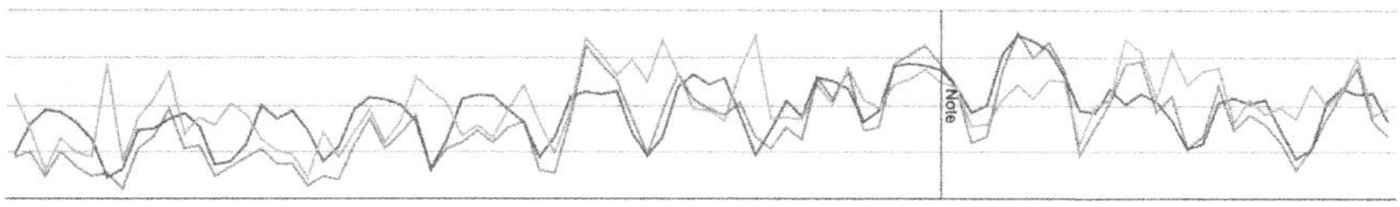

	Queries	Monthly Volume	CPC	Competition	Clicks ▾	Impressions	CTR	
1	roadmap				1,235	37,497	3.29%	»
2	road map				534	30,283	1.76%	»
3	roadmap space				38	63	60.32%	»
4	roadmap.space	0	$0.00	0	22	28	78.57%	»
5	roadmap saas	0	$0.00	0	11	75	14.67%	»
6	rod map	90,500	$0.10	0.35	6	180	3.33%	»
7	github roadmap tool	10	$3.67	0.59	4	21	19.05%	»

The first thing I do on this screen (especially for startups) is I change the date range to 90 days.

Next, I'll take a look at which search terms generate the most clicks to their website. Roadmap is getting most of their clicks from the keyword "roadmap."

Besides Clicks, we also want to look at the number of Impressions a search term is getting, and the click-through rates.

One potential challenge with the word "roadmap" is that some folks are using that keyword to get a map with driving directions (as opposed to a product roadmap).

So let's see what Google is returning when we search "roadmap."

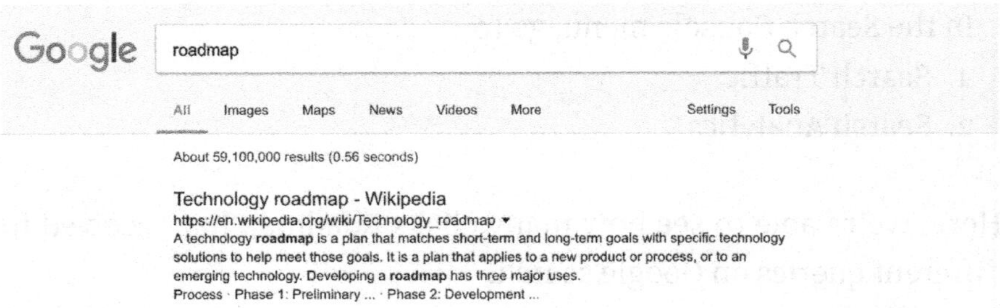

The results are encouraging: a Wikipedia article on "technology roadmap" is the first result.

We're also getting a sense of what Google thinks is important. They're highlighting questions like: "what is on a road map?" and "what is a product roadmap in Agile development?"

Additionally, we can see which products are ranking highly for that term. There's one called ppmroadmap.com, and another called wrike.com.

Finally, there are the "searches related to" our keyword (roadmap). Here we see keyword combinations like "roadmap template," "roadmap project management," and "roadmap app."

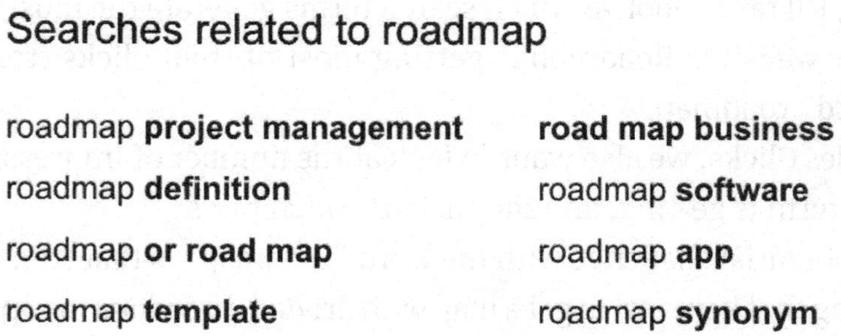

By default, Google personalizes your search results based on your location and your Google account information. You can depersonalize your search results by adding this string *&pws=0&gl=us* to your query.

For example:

*google.com/search?q=roadmap**&pws=0&gl=us***

Here's how it works:

- &pws=0 – removes any personalized search results.
- &gl=us – changes my region to the USA.

The next tool we're going to use is called WooRank. It generates an SEO report that looks like this:

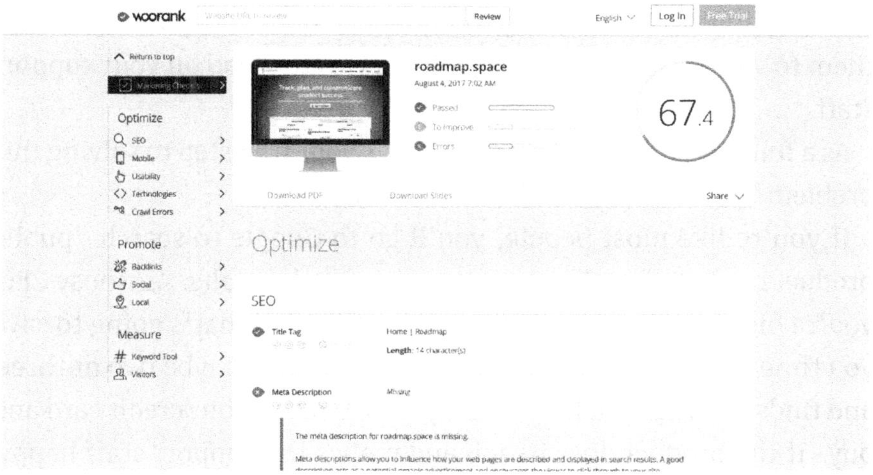

It highlights some opportunities for things we could fix:

- The title tag currently says "Home | Roadmap" and isn't optimized for search. For example, we could change that to "Product Roadmaps for Startups."
- The site is also missing a meta description.

- The headings (h1, h2, h3) don't describe the product or use focus keywords.
- In the keyword cloud, we can see the word "roadmap" comes up the most frequently. However, the next most mentioned terms are "feedback," "users," and "pricing." We can improve this!

The research we've done here is important. It gives us a feel for where Roadmap is now and where they need to go. Now we can see the SEO opportunities.

Finding keywords for your website

I want you to imagine that you're a startup founder talking to your VP of customer success, just chatting, and he mentions that users want to see your product roadmap. They have questions about which features you're going to release next, and because there's no public place for them to view that information, it increases the load on your support staff.

As a founder, what will you do? What's your first step to solving this problem?

If you're like most people, you'll go to Google to search "public product roadmap" and get a long list of search results. As a busy CEO, you're highly incentivized to pay for something that's going to save you time and money. You try out a few options, maybe two or three, and finds one that you like. Then, you'll take out your credit card and buy. If the product does its job and makes the support staff happy, you'll feel like it was a good purchase. You'll feel like you've made progress.

That's how most sales happen on the web.

Let's go back to our case study, Roadmap. In the last section, we identified some key opportunities. Using WooRank and Google's Search Console, we saw what people are already searching and what the click-through rate was.

ahrefs.com

Now we need to figure out what keywords we should target (and fix problems with the title tag, meta description, headings). I'm going to start by using a tool called ahrefs.com. Here's what the process is going to look like:

1. Type in your website. In our case, this is roadmap.space.
2. We need to start thinking about which keywords we want. Things like "roadmap" and "product roadmap" and "public product roadmap." Then we can look at their suggestions to get some more keywords like "slack roadmap." Also, make sure to spell things correctly.
3. We have to enter in some countries. In our case, all we need to choose is "United States."
4. We need to add some competitors. For us, this will be Trello, User Voice, ProdPlan, and maybe Roadmap Planner.
5. Submit to receive the report.

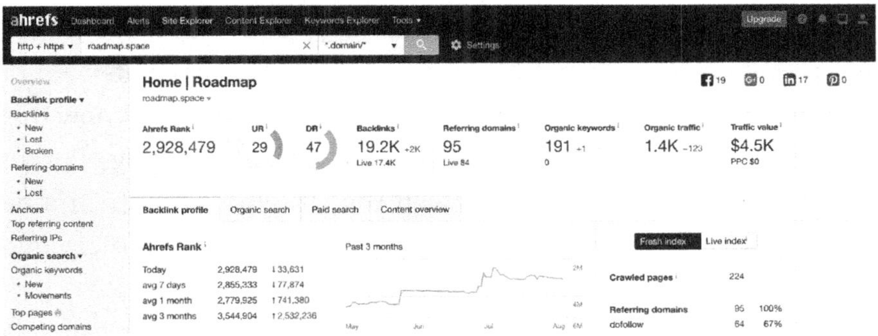

There's a lot to show you here; here are a few highlights.

First, is going to be competing domains. These are the domains of your competitors. We can open the data on any of the competitors to look at their organic keywords.

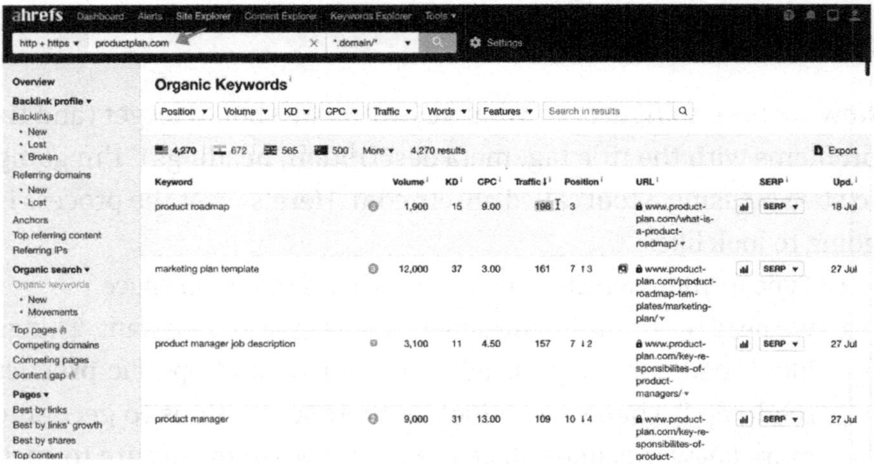

We can see that productplan.com is number three for "product roadmap" and getting a fair amount of traffic for it. As we dig a little deeper, we find that search volume and clicks are increasing for that keyword.

In this case, the keyword difficulty for "product roadmap" is low. This is good news! It means we'll likely need backlinks from about six websites to rank in the top ten for this term.

When we look at backlinks for Roadmap, we can see most of their referrals are coming from Designer News and Product Hunt.

But if we look at the backlinks for productplan.com, we know they have way more backlinks from sites like the Buffer blog, Forbes, Medium, Entrepreneur.com, as well the UK government. It's becoming apparent why productplan.com is number three for "product roadmap."

ahrefs.com also gives us some search suggestions for other keywords we might want to target, like "product roadmap template" and "product roadmap software." Remember, you can also see those kinds of suggestions if you just search for your keyword and go to the bottom of the first page ("searches related to").

Ahrefs also suggests other search terms, like "product strategy" or "definition of product." I like to take these suggestions and put them into a text file called "keyword ideas."

Answer the Public

Answer the Public is another helpful tool for browsing words and coming up with keyword suggestions. When I type in "product roadmap" I get a visualization like this:

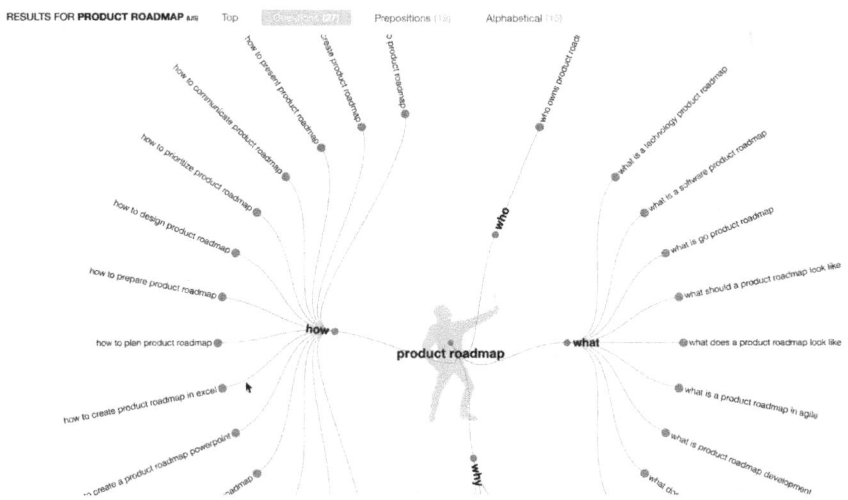

What I like about this is it visualizes the main keyword, but then shows you all the questions people are asking about the topic. For example, "Who owns the product roadmap?" or "What is a technology roadmap?" or "What is a software product roadmap?" You can click on any of these, and it will take you to that actual search, where you can see who's ranking and what content Google is scraping.

If we scroll down to the Prepositions section, we get even more ideas. Things like:

- "roadmap for products"
- "roadmap for product launch"

- "roadmap for product development"
- "product roadmap how to"
- "product roadmap with JIRA"
- "product roadmap with Trello."

All of these keywords are ideas we can add to our "keyword ideas" text file.

Google Trends

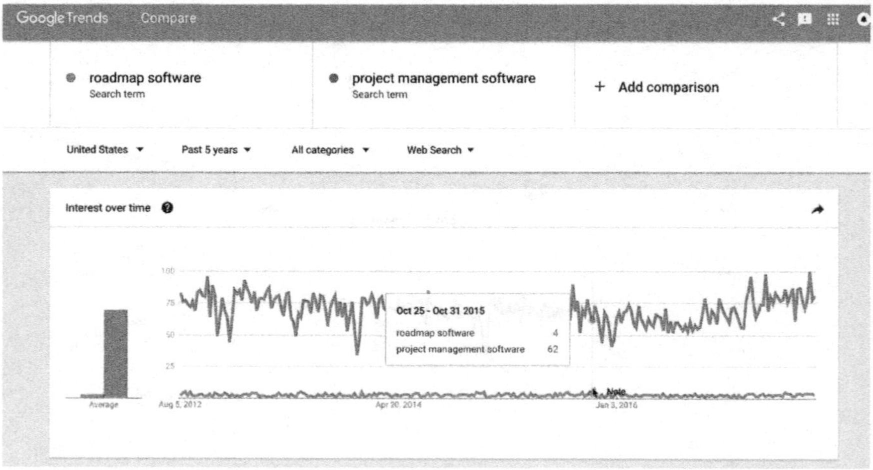

I want to show you one more tool that can be helpful in this whole process. Google Trends shows you relative search interest for different keywords. For example, if we put in the term "roadmap software" it would plot the interest over time. We can now compare this keyword to other queries to gain insights:

1. There is more interest in "project management" than "roadmap."
2. The term "project management software" is much more popular than "roadmap software."

Fix your website's SEO problems

Next, let's look at editing our homepage page content so we can target the keywords we just discovered.

Title

The first thing we need to fix is the title tag. The title tag says "Home" and then "Roadmap," and doesn't tell people anything about the product.

Going back to our keyword planner, we can see that "product roadmap" is a high-interest keyword, so that's what we're going to add. I'm going to change the title to "Product roadmap software."

Meta Description

The meta description is a summary of your web page's content. It should be shorter than 160 characters. For Roadmap's meta description I wrote: "product roadmap software and tools for startups." I also identified some meta keywords: "roadmap," "roadmap software," and "roadmap tools."

```
<title>Product roadmap software | Roadmap</title>
<!-- This site is optimized with the Yoast SEO plugin v4.0.2 - https://yoast.com/wordpre
<link rel="canonical" href="https://roadmap.space/">
<!-- Basic metadata -->
<meta name="description" content="Product roadmap software and tools for startups">
<meta name="keywords" content="roadmap, roadmap software, roadmap tools, public product
```

Content Optimization

Next, let's edit the homepage's text. When you optimize your content for search engines you get an added advantage: it also makes the page more readable.

1. Headline

I'm going to change the current headline of "planning software for startups" to "product roadmap software."

2. Sub-Headline

For the sub-headline, we might say something like, "tools for product managers, founders, and software teams."

3. Section Headlines

As we scroll down, we might find some other titles. Search engines pay particular attention to H1, H2, and H3 tags, so we may want to add keywords in there, such as "Roadmap features."

4. Alt Text

Defining the "alt text" tags for your images is also important for SEO. The alt tag was designed to show text when an image is not loading correctly, or if someone is using a screen reader. Google indexes alt text, so put relevant keywords in these descriptions!

Review

After finishing homepage edits, I like to look at my list of keywords again to make sure I used them all.

These little content tweaks on your homepage (and other pages) should gradually improve your search results over time.

SEO for Wordpress

If you want to make your SEO activities simpler, I recommend you use a WordPress plugin called Yoast. There are a few reasons I recommend this.

1. It helps optimize your focus keyword

What's a focus keyword? Yoast describes it like this:

> *The focus keyword is the keyword that you want your page to rank for, so when people search for that keyword, they'll find you.*

In Yoast, you enter in the focus keyword, and it analyzes your content.

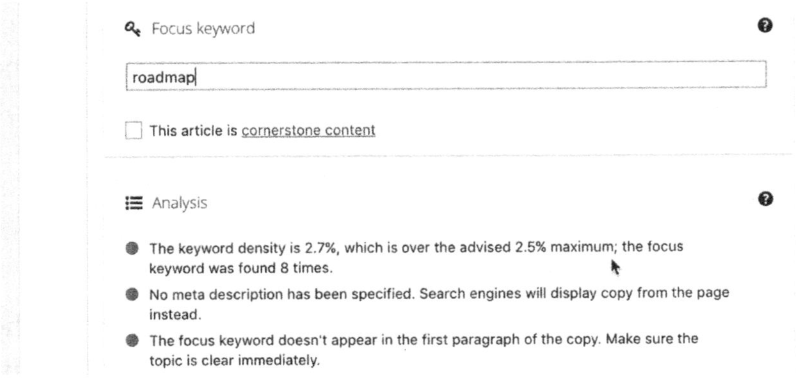

In this case, Yoast is recommending we reduce the number of times we say "roadmap" on the page. It's also noticed that we don't have a meta description and gives us an easy way to update it.

2. Edit Google search results copy

Yoast also provides a preview of what the page will look like in Google search results. Here we can see that "Home | Roadmap" is not a great title.

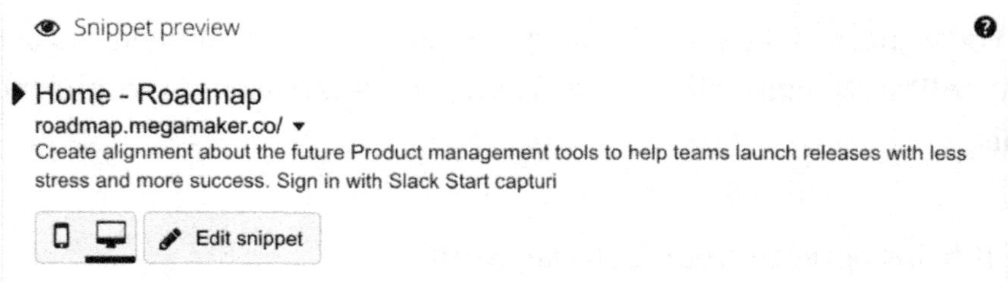

Also, because there is no meta description specified, Google displays the first lines of text on the page. In Yoast, we can define a search-friendly title and description.

3. Adjust for social

Although not specifically related to SEO, Yoast also gives us a preview of what our site would look like in social media posts. Now is a good time to make sure your feature image looks good in tweets and Facebook posts.

Creating Content

The home page is an important piece, but even more important are the landing pages and blog posts you're going to create on your domain. Now is the time to use Answer the Public. If I type in "roadmap," we're going to get all the questions and propositions related to that term.

Example 1

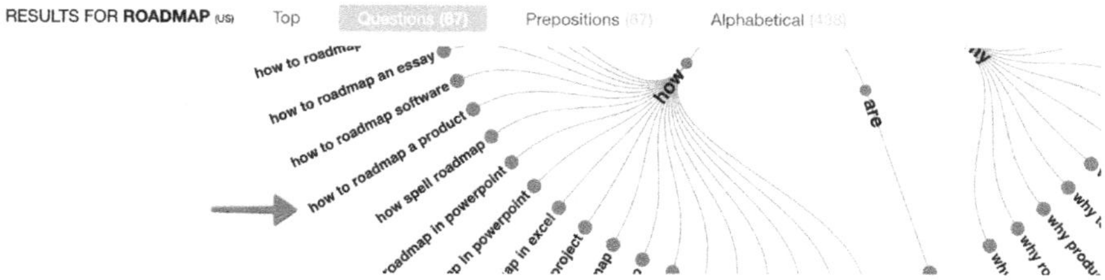

"How to roadmap a product" would make a great blog post, so I'm going to head back into WordPress and make that the title of a new blog post. Here are some things I might include in the post as I write:

- show an example of a product roadmap
- a quick list of tips for building a product roadmap

After writing, Yoast is going to help us optimize the post for search. When we type in our focus keyword, "how to roadmap product," Yoast gives us some suggestions. For example, the focus keyword doesn't appear in the first paragraph. That's an easy win, so we'll add a new section and make sure to include the keyword.

We'll also make other changes, like editing the meta description and ensuring the post will look right on Twitter and Facebook.

Example 2

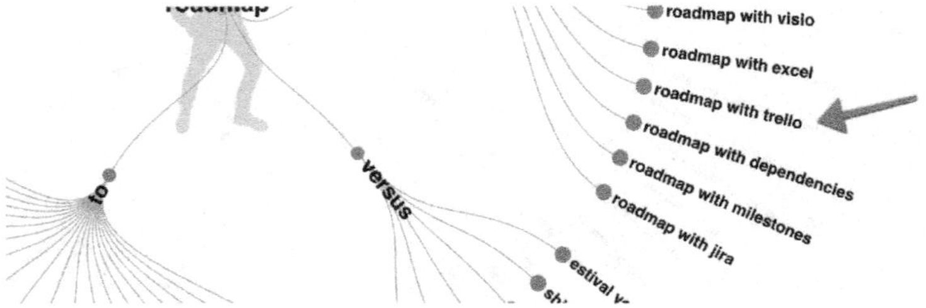

Lower down in our Answer the Public results, we find "product roadmap with Trello." That's another great blog post topic. In this case, I would create a blog post called "How to create a product roadmap with Trello." I'd define my focus keyword as "Trello roadmap."

Review

Using WordPress and Yoast together makes improving your search results feel like a game. As you write in WordPress, you'll try to increase the SEO score that Yoast gives you.

It also gives you all the tools are in one place: readability, keyword suggestions, social media previews. Yoast will also generate a sitemap that you can submit to Google Search Console.

21

Get more leads

After you launch, your biggest need will be filling the top of your marketing funnel with leads. Here are some tactics to get your started.

Email the people you know

For his new product, Drip, Rob Walling emailed 17 founders. These were people he knew, like Crazy Egg's Hiten Shah. In his email, Rob asked a specific question:

> *I don't want you to tell me that you think this is an interesting idea; I want to know if you would actually use and pay for it.*

Building relationships with people in your target audience, and then emailing them, is an excellent way to get your first customers.

This approach applies to products that have already launched as well. Write a personal email that looks something like this:

> *Hi [name],*
>
> *We've known each other since we met at [location] in [year]. It's been fascinating to see your business, [business name], grow over the years.*

As you know, I've been working on [my product]. The aim is to help business owners [value proposition].

Do you already have a solution for this? If not, I'd love to give you a free trial for [my product].

If you're already using something, let me know. It'd be great for you to take a look at [my product] and tell me what might help you switch.

Cheers,
[your name]

Always be building relationships! You can't build a network overnight, but here are some unique ways to meet new people and get out of your comfort zone:

1. Buy someone lunch

There was a CEO that I wanted to meet, but I was never able to connect with him at social events. So I wrote him an email with the subject line: "Can I buy you lunch?" In the email, I said, "You're a business leader that I respect. I want to get better at *x*. Can I take you for lunch?" He replied and said, "I'd love to go for lunch, but you don't have to buy."

Everyone likes going to lunch. Be generous, and you could receive enjoyable company, and great advice, in return.

2. Start a podcast

This one isn't for everyone, but I've been able to have amazing conversations with interesting people through my podcasts (Build & Launch, Product People). Podcasts are great because they give you a good reason to have a conversation with interesting people. Most folks are flattered when you invite them to be a guest on your show.

You don't need to be naturally outgoing or extroverted to record a podcast. Some of the best hosts I know are the opposite!

3. Start a meetup

My friends Kevin and Jared didn't like the other networking events in town, so they decided to start their own: Nerds Night Out. Instead of doing the "normal" thing and have a presenter, they just get together for drinks at a pub. They started small by inviting a few other people in the web development community. It gradually grew, and now 10–25 people come each month.

4. Take a class; in a different city

One way to meet a whole new group of people is to take a class in a different city. I went to a Ruby Weekend in Las Vegas. It was actually easier meeting people as the out-of-towner because I was unique (I was the only non-local). I still keep in touch with people from this class.

5. Volunteer at an event

Every event organizer needs help: a photographer, a sound person, a host (to welcome people). When you volunteer, you get to meet the organizing team, and anyone attending the event. (Plus, you usually get to attend and participate for free.)

5. Go to a conference, and look for ways to help

My friend, Mike Bridge, goes to events and takes photos. When he takes pictures of attendees and speakers, he offers to email people their photographs.

When Kai Davis attended MicroConf, he took detailed notes from each speaker's presentation and offered to send them to attendees.[39]

These are great techniques: they help you make meaningful connections and provide you with an excuse to follow up with people.

Email people you don't know

Before he'd even built WPEngine, Jason Cohen talked to 50 people and asked them if they would pay $50 each month for stable WordPress hosting. Then he asked them for a cheque towards their first month. In his 2012 interview on Mixergy[40], he explained his process:

> *Anyone can do this. You go to LinkedIn, and you search for the type of person that you want to interview. I found people who were professionals, that is, they charge money for their time. Then, I contacted every one of them, which is easy, since, as they are consultants you can find them, and their email addresses and they answer it because that's their sales line. So, it's very easy to contact people who are professionals in the field. So, I would send an email to each one, and this is what I'd say exactly. I'd say, "Hey, we're thinking of building these new tools for WordPress. You are exactly the kind of person who we'd want to use these tools. I would love to get your opinion." Here's the result, 100% of them agreed to the interview.*

Jason used this tactic to validate his idea before launching, but you can use it to find customers after launching as well. One key is Jason offered to compensate them for their time. He knew that some of these professionals charge $200 per hour, but he was willing to pay because it showed respect to the consultant. Interestingly, not one person took

---

[39] http://doubleyouraudience.com/microconf/

[40] WP Engine: How A Startup Reached $1M in Sales in Less Than a Year - with Jason Cohen, Mixergy, 2012

him up on his offer.

Ask for referrals

Using the previous two techniques, you should be able to get your first five customers. What do you do now?

Ask those customers for referrals! Make it an automatic process for every new client. Once they're using your product, send them an email like this:

> *Hi [name],*
>
> *It looks like you've been using [my product] for a couple of weeks now! Thank you, I'm glad to have you as a customer.*
>
> *You seem like you're well connected in the [industry name] circles. Do you know anyone that could benefit from [my product]?*
>
> *If so, could introduce them to me? I've attached a template you can use to email them.*
>
> *Cheers,*
> *[your name]*

Having the above conversation over the phone might be even more powerful. The key is to ask.

Many people get uncomfortable asking for referrals. Steli Efti, the founder of Close.io, thinks they're missing out on a tremendous opportunity:[41]

> *Referral sales can be your #1 source of new leads and turn into a*

[41] http://blog.close.io/how-to-do-referral-sales

massive growth engine for your B2B startup if you do it right. Why are so many sales people doing referral sales wrong? Because they're afraid. It's scary to ask for more once you close a deal. Sales people worry that they might jeopardize a deal, or that it'll turn a positive conversation awkward. Go where others are afraid to go, and you'll find massive opportunity. Don't let fear get in the way.

Don't complicate this by implementing an affiliate scheme, or trying to reward customers for their referrals. Most satisfied customers are happy to do this for you. They don't want payment.

Give away a free eBook that gets people hooked

You have a great product, but it's likely behind a paywall. For people to experience it, and benefit from it, they need to pay first.

One way to get people on your email list is to give them a little taste of the benefit your product offers in content form.

Intercom provides software that allows companies to talk to their customers. They offer a free, high-quality ebook on Product Management that anyone can download for free:

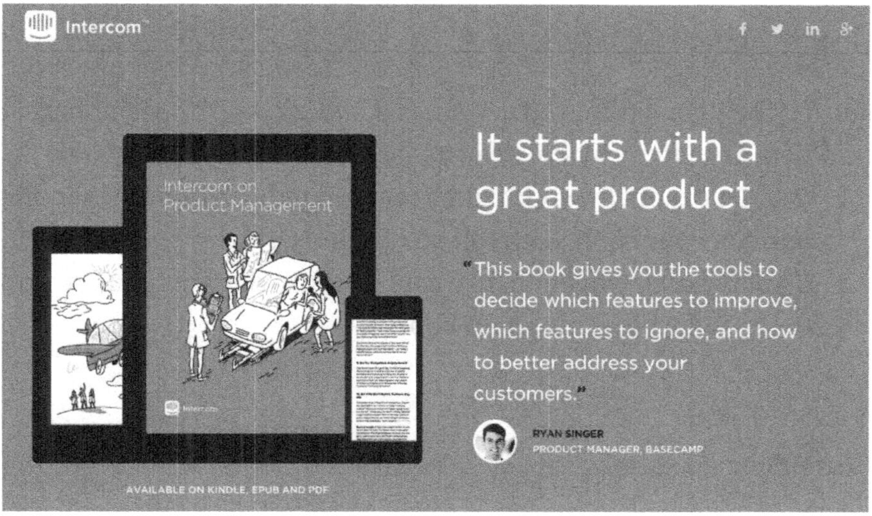

To attract more subscribers, Intercom developed a free ebook

To get the book, you need to enter your email address:

To get the free book, you need to enter your email address

Finding content for an eBook

Putting together a whole book sounds daunting, but it doesn't have to be. There are a few ways you can get great content for your book:

1. Ask ten experts in your field if you can publish one of their blog posts in your book, with full attribution.
2. If you've been blogging, take your ten best blog posts and rewrite them as ten essays for your book.

Assembling an ebook

Once you have your content, you need to get it into ebook form. At a minimum, this means creating a PDF that people can download and read on their computer or tablet. If you want to go the extra mile, you can also offer it in ePub and MOBI.

The easiest way to export an attractive PDF ebook is with Apple's iBooks Author. It's free, has great templates and layout options, and is relatively easy to use.

Here are some other options:

- Softcover – if you're a Ruby on Rails developer, you'll love their take on publishing.
- Reedsy – a web application that helps you write and publish your ebook. I used it to write and publish this book!
- Pressbooks – allows you to publish PDF, MOBI, and ePub books from WordPress.

Delivering the book to subscribers

So the user flow is going to look like this:

1. Someone visits your homepage, landing page or blog.
2. On the page, you have a call to action (similar to Intercom's above)

that asks the visitor if they want to get your ebook (free).
3. They enter their email address.
4. Your email system automatically sends them an email asking them to confirm their address. To download the book, the subscriber clicks the confirmation link.

There are a few different tools you can use for this:

- **MailChimp.com:** You can add a file to the final welcome email, or (if you're using Automation) you can add a file to one of your triggered emails.[42]
- **Gumroad.com:** You can create a free product in Gumroad, and add your ebook files to it. People go to the Gumroad landing page, click the "I want this" button, and are asked to enter their email address. Alternatively, you could use their Audience feature and set up a Workflow that automatically sends them your ebook when they subscribe.
- **ConvertKit.com:** ConvertKit was built expressly for this use-case. You create a subscription form in ConvertKit and upload your PDF. A subscriber automatically receives a welcome email with the download link.

Write a surprising blog post that gets people interested

Don't underestimate the value of creating something unexpected, unusual, and weird: these are the blog posts that get read and shared.

Derek Sivers[43] is one of my favorite bloggers of all time. When I asked him for writing advice he said:

> *Before you publish, ask, "What is surprising about this?" If it's*

---

[42] Send a File to New Subscribers, MailChimp

[43] sivers.org

not surprising, then you're not telling them anything they don't already know. If it's not surprising yet, look for the surprising element. Think of a way that this idea can be really helpful to people.

Sacha Greif (co-author of *Discover Meteor*) is great at writing these types of posts. Check out his piece *What Kind of Logo Do You Get for $5?*

This title, by Sacha Greif, already hints that something surprising is coming

In it, Sacha compares the type of work you would get from his service, Folyo, to what you would get for $5 from Fiverr. There are all sorts of unexpected gems in the piece, including bits like this under the headline "Bait & Switch":

> *After noticing this pattern, the explanation became clear: these designers were appropriating other designers' work, and passing it off as their own. This little switcheroo is a big no-no in the design community, and it's obviously quite misleading for prospective clients as well. It seemed to be standard practice on Fiverr.*

These are the type of "ah-ha!" moments that people love to share.

Create a free tool that naturally leads to your paid product

Reuben Gamez has a lead magnet that helps him attract thousands of customers. His SaaS product, Bidsketch, gives away free downloadable templates.[44]

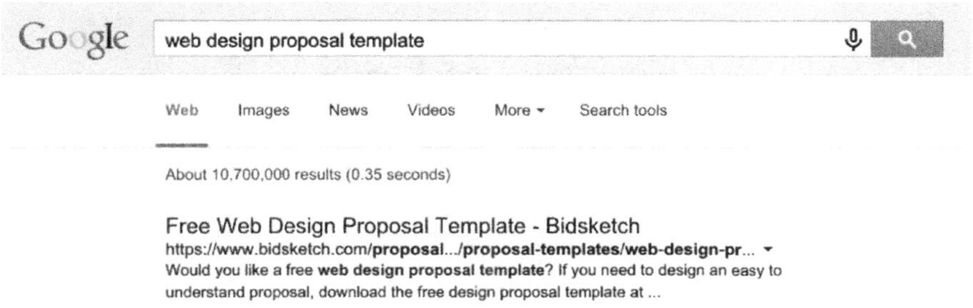

Google "web design proposal template." Who is at the top of the list?

When you search for "web design proposal template" on Google, the first result is a landing page on Bidsketch. It's filled with great advice ("Demonstrate you understand their problems with a Problem Statement"), and research bits like this:

> *Our research shows that online proposals are accepted 60% faster than traditional proposals, and they're 18% more likely to be accepted overall.*

Finally, at the bottom of the page, the reader has a chance to enter their email and get free templates sent to their email address:

[44] https://www.bidsketch.com/proposal-resources/proposal-templates/

After giving great information on screen, the reader can get the templates sent to their inbox

Moments later, an email pops up in the prospect's inbox. It has a download link to a zip file that contains two proposal templates (in Word, Pages, and InDesign formats). The templates are high quality and could easily save a freelancer hours of work. But if a freelancer wants an automated, online solution for creating proposals, they know where to go: Bidsketch.

Have a point of view that gets people talking

From the beginning, it was clear that Basecamp's Jason Fried and David Heinemeier Hansson had strong opinions. In their book, Rework, they spell it out:

> *Great businesses have a point of view, not just a product or service. You have to believe in something. A strong stand is how you attract superfans. They spread the word further, wider, and more*

passionately than any advertising could.

Not everyone likes Basecamp. But the founders have drawn a line in the sand: they're clear about what they believe in.

A point of view invites discussion: "Can you believe they said this?" "What do you think about this?" "I agree with them."

Share your process

When Alex Turnball started Groove, he knew he wanted to do things differently than he had with his first company, Bantam Live. Groove is help desk software for small businesses.

Instead of buying ads or starting an affiliate program, Alex decided they would publicly share Groove's journey from $28,525 to $100,000 in monthly revenue.[45]

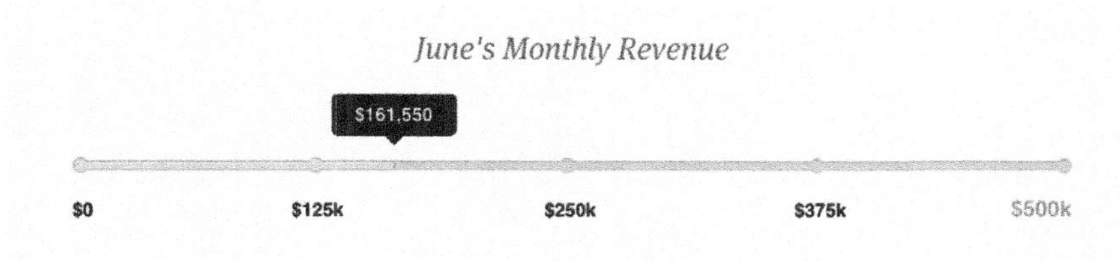

Groove made their revenue numbers transparent

In 14 months, the Groove team wrote over 50 blog posts detailing the tactics they used (and the lessons they learned) to get to $100k in recurring revenue. People responded to it in a big way. Over 30,000 people signed up to get regular updates on the company's progress.

[45] https://www.groovehq.com/blog/100k

The next step

A lead is a potential customer: someone who has the intent to buy and the budget to do so. Someone knowing about your product isn't enough. Nurture your leads from initial contact through a series of steps up until the purchase. In the next chapter, we'll look at the sales funnel and how you can keep your leads engaged.

22

Guide your leads through the funnel

Getting people to visit your website is hard enough. The trouble is, once people visit and leave, there's no way to stay in touch with them.

Every business has a funnel that describes how people go from being the target market to becoming customers. Funnels look something like this:

Traditional online marketing funnel

People rarely become a lead on their first visit to a website, and trial users don't always convert immediately.

It's helpful to think about the *timeline* behind a purchase. The folks at Jobs to Be Done[46] have one that looks like this:

[46] jobstobedone.org

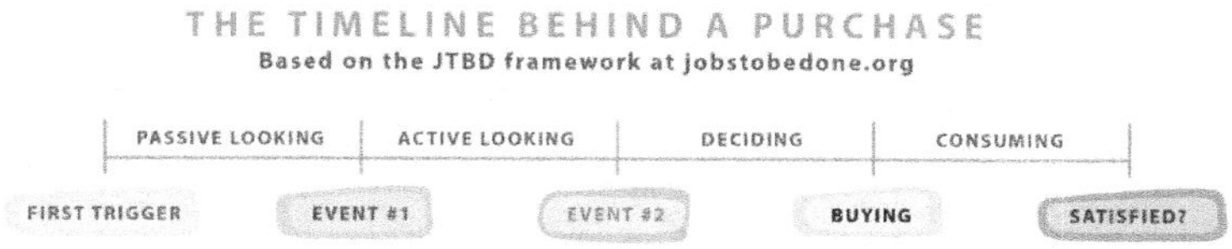

A purchaser goes through different phases before she buys

You attract people during the *passive looking* stage (that was the previous chapter). They hopefully visit your website during the *active looking* step. Now, you have to guide them through the *deciding* phase.

Some decisions happen in an instant: "I heard this Android app is popular, I'm going to buy it now." Others can take months (think enterprise software).

Tweetbot is my favorite Twitter app for the iPhone. I heard about it in 2011. When I visited the website, I left without buying. However, I kept hearing people talk about Tweetbot; mostly on podcasts. Sometimes these were paid advertisements, but other times it was because the hosts were gushing about how much they loved it. One day Twitter updated their official app to show more ads in the timeline. I decided I'd had enough and bought Tweetbot for $4.99. The year? 2014. It took me *three years* from initial contact to actual purchase.

This goes contrary to much of our thinking about marketing. Most of us believe that people see an ad for our product and instantly go and buy.

Most purchases don't work this way

Most products (even apps) require that you nurture your leads. Nurturing leads requires that you capture some information about people who view your product, and use that information to remind that your product exists!

Here are some ways to guide your leads toward a purchase.

Write an email course

My best conversion rates come from a 5-part email course. What's an email course? It's an automated sequence of emails that you drip out daily or weekly. The idea is that you give the reader an easily digested lesson in each email.

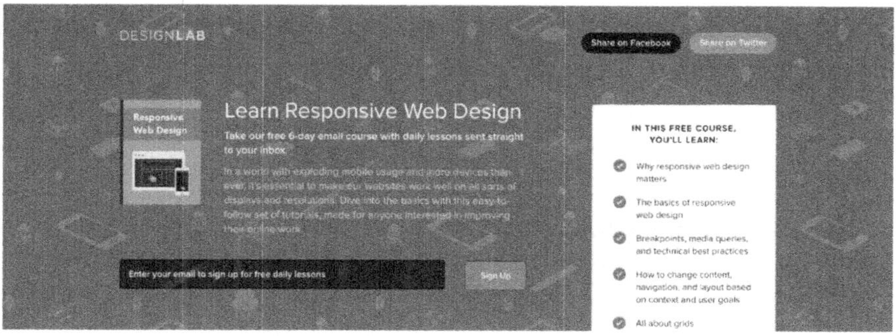

trydesignlab.com/responsive-web-design/

Structure the content for your email course

Email courses work best if they're 5–7 days of content. Most email courses are daily: you subscribe and get lesson 1, and then the subsequent lessons come each day after that.

You may already have content written that you can use for an email course:

1. Break up a long, tactical article or white paper into five lessons.
2. Already have a blog series on a topic? Convert each post into a lesson!
3. Ask people for questions on Twitter or by email, and turn your answers into email lessons.

How do email courses help nurture your leads?

Each day, you're giving the subscriber something valuable. This builds trust and rapport with the prospect. Your lessons should also naturally lead to your product.

For example, in one lesson you might describe a DIY approach to solving a problem. The email outlines all the steps they would need to take to do it themselves. At the end of the email, you explain that there's an easier way: your product. This is exactly the approach that Bidsketch's Reuben Gamez uses in his course:

> Your proposals.
>
> Most often, you're getting plenty of leads, but you're losing too many of them at the proposal stage. And almost always, it's because the proposal does not get straight to the point.
>
> The good news is, this is an amazingly easy fix. And with a simple templating system like Bidsketch, it's a change you only have to make once.
>
> More here:
>
> www.bidsketch.com

The end of Reuben's Bidsketch email

Delivering an email course to subscribers

The user flow is going to look like this:

1. Someone visits your homepage, landing page or blog.
2. On the page, you have a call to action (similar to Design Lab's above) that asks the visitor if they want to subscribe to get 5–7 lessons by email.
3. They enter their email address.
4. Your email system automatically sends them the first lesson in your drip sequence. Every day following, the subscriber receives an email.

There are a few different tools you can use to create email courses:

MailChimp

MailChimp recently released their automation feature to all users. Automation allows you to create drip sequences easily.[47] Their drag and drop interface for arranging lessons is particularly helpful.

ConvertKit

ConvertKit has email courses baked right into their primary service. When you create a new course you're given an email sequence template to edit:

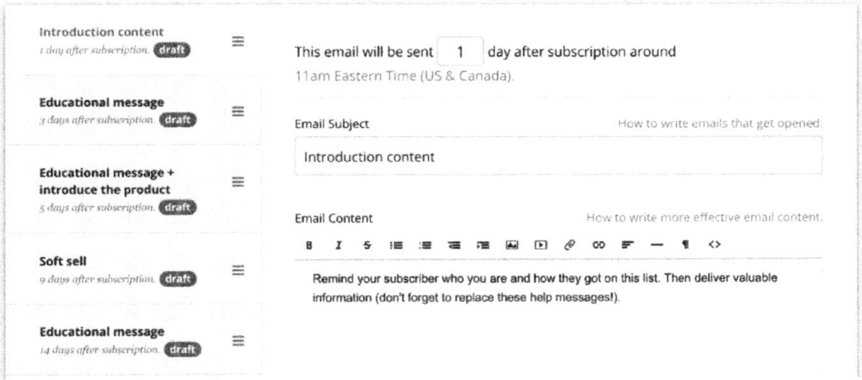

ConvertKit has pre-made email course templates

Current pricing for ConvertKit starts at $29 for up to 1,000 subscribers. Their target market is professional bloggers, so if you're building an info-product, they might be a good fit.

The team there has steadily increased the app's automation functionality. You can now tag subscribers and trigger event automation with link clicks, purchase events, or subscription events.

---

47 http://mailchimp.com/features/automation/

Drip

I've tried all four of the email marketing tools here, and Drip is the most robust (especially for those with SaaS products). Conversion tracking is built in, allowing you to see if your course is resulting in more customers.

Drip's campaign reports include conversion tracking

Drip also has my favorite subscription widget: it's a little tab that sits on the bottom right-hand side of your website and pops open after a timed delay.

For some of my SaaS clients, we've achieved 30% visit-to-trial conversion rates using Drip's system.

Use retargeting ads

How does retargeting work? When a visitor comes to your website, your site drops an anonymous cookie in their browser. When the visitor leaves, they start seeing your ads on Facebook, on Google, or even on mobile apps.

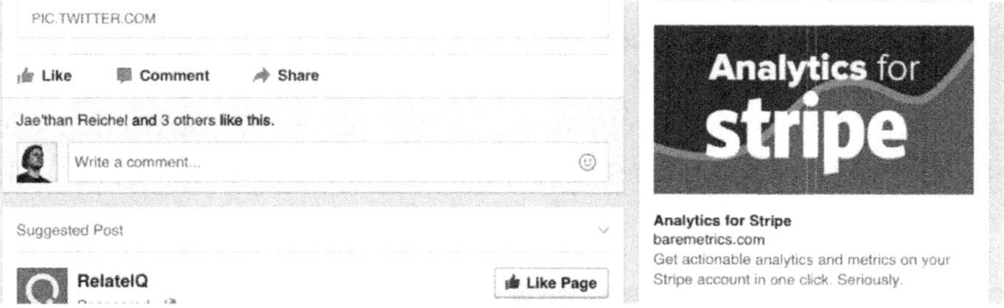

Guess whose website I visited right before going to Facebook?

Retargeting (or "remarketing" as Google calls it), is a way to remind people of your product, long after they've left your web page.

Start on Facebook

The easiest way to get started with retargeting is on Facebook's ad platform. They've developed good tools for building ads, and most campaigns are approved with minutes of being launched.

Step 1: Sign up

1. Go to facebook.com/business and click "Create an ad."
2. Choose either "Increase conversions on your website" or "Get installs of your app" (if you have a mobile app).
3. Facebook will ask you to install a conversion tracking pixel on your site. In most cases, you'll add it to the purchase confirmation page (or newsletter sign-up confirmation page). Example: /thank-you.html
4. Next, give your campaign a name. Remember, a campaign can have multiple sets of ads, so it's best to be general.

Step 2: Create an audience

In step 2 of Facebook's ad creation process, they'll ask you to choose an audience. Click the *Create Custom Audience* link, and you'll be brought to this screen:

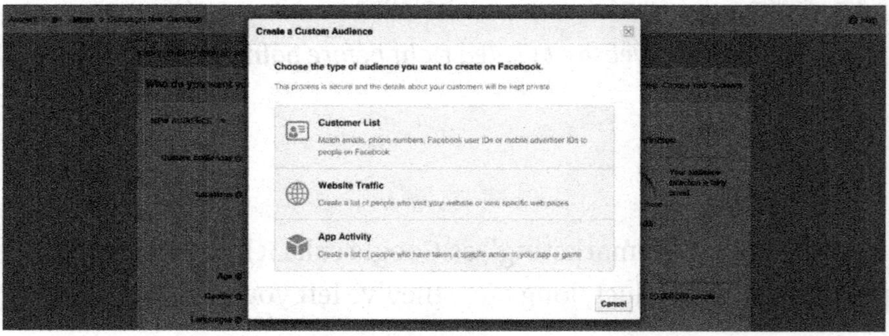

Facebook offers three types of retargeting

We're going to start with *Website Traffic*. When you click that option, you'll be asked to install another snippet on your website, a "custom audience pixel."

Next, you'll define how much of your traffic you want to track for retargeting. If your traffic is low, you may want to track the last 60–90 days (you can go up to 180 days).

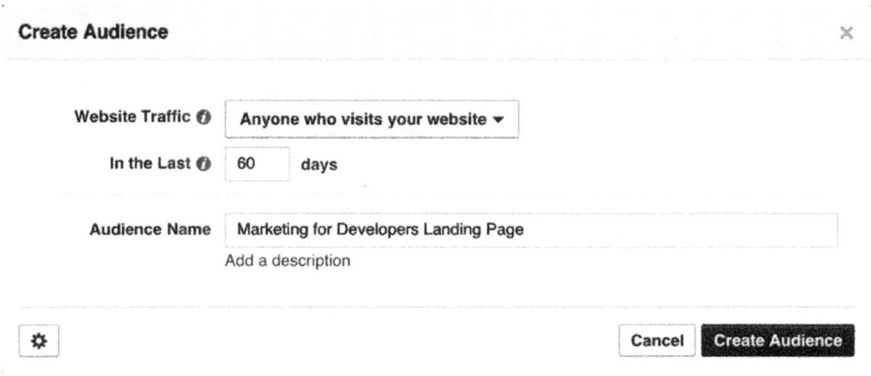

Define the parameters

At this point, you haven't cookied any of your website visitors with Facebook's tracking pixel, so you won't be able to target them quite yet. You can either wait for that to happen or create other retargeting audiences.

You can also have Facebook match your email subscribers. They have billions of email addresses hashed in their system: when you upload your list, they hash your addresses and then match the hashes. To upload a list, click the *Create Custom Audience* link again. You can connect directly to MailChimp (if you're using that) or upload a CSV.

Step 3: Define your budget

You enter your budget details in this screen here:

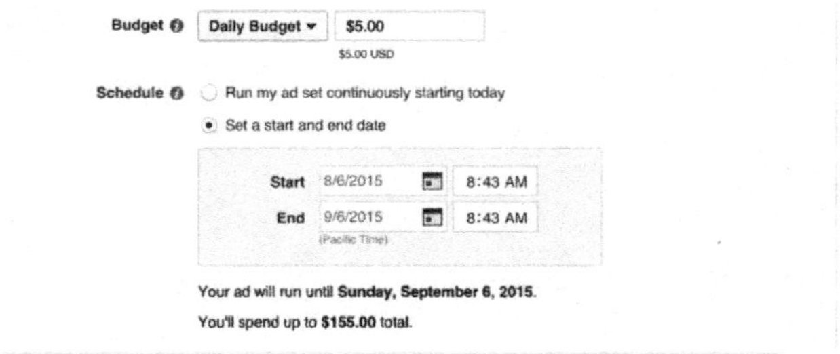

Facebook will show you how much you'll spend

Now you'll need to decide how much you can spend. There are two different approaches I'd advocate here:

1. **Set it and forget it**: if you can't spend time tweaking ads as they run, I'd allocate $150 for 30 days ($5 per day).
2. **Focused week-long test:** if you're able to dedicate some time and resources to your ad campaign, try upping your daily budget to $25–$100. Keep a close eye on it! If, after a day, you're not getting the conversions you want, kill that ad variation and try another one. Repeat the process over 5–7 days until you find something that works.

Step 4: Create your ad

Once you have a big enough audience, you can create your ad variations. Here are a few choices you'll need to make:

- **Display a single image or multiple images?** If you'd like to show a series of screenshots, you can show a carousel of five images in your ad. Otherwise, you can have your ad feature a single image or video.
- **Image variations:** For each campaign, I'd recommend uploading multiple images. Each image you upload will create a new variation on your ad. Facebook will track the effectiveness of each image and will automatically start showing the best-converting image

for you.

- **Text and links:** You'll also need to write your ad copy. The most effective ads focus on the struggle: "Ambassador makes referral programs easy." Or center on the solution: "Get your theatre tickets instantly."
- **What variations you'll run:** You can run your ads on *Facebook's Desktop Newsfeed* (the main column in Facebook), the *Mobile Newsfeed*, *Desktop Right Column*, and *Audience Network.* If you have a SaaS product or an informational product (like an ebook or a course) I would focus on the *Desktop Newsfeed* and *Right Column* only. Mobile apps should focus on *Mobile Newsfeed.* Don't use the *Audience Network.*

Choose where your ads will run on Facebook

With this last step done, you can place your order. It usually takes a few hours for Facebook to approve your ads.

Step 5: Evaluate your campaign

To properly evaluate your campaign, you're going to need to determine the lifetime value (LTV) of a customer. If you have a mobile app, your lifetime value might be 99 cents. If you have a SaaS, it might be $480 ($20 x 24 months).

Now, look at your *Performance* graph in Facebook Ads:

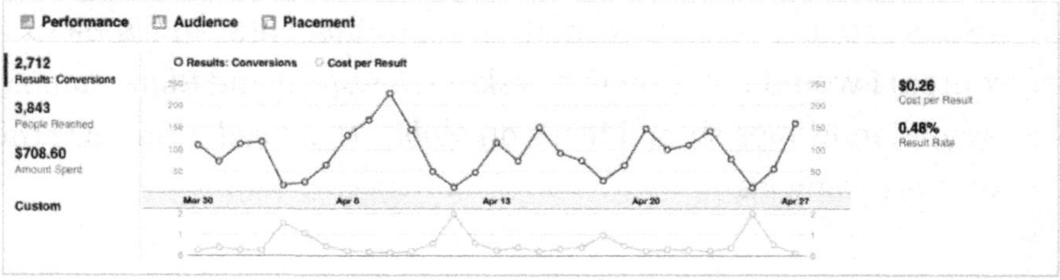

Facebook ads performance graph

This will show you the number of conversions you achieved over time and how much it cost to get them. If you're selling a mobile app where you receive $0.99 on every unit, and your *cost per result* is $0.26, you've made $0.73 on average per sale. That's a decent return on investment. Conversions from retargeted ads usually cost less than regular ads.

You should keep advertising if the cost of acquiring the customer is cheaper than your sale price. Finding an ad channel that works is difficult, but when you find one it allows you to double-down and easily earn more income.

Facebook will also give you demographic information on who is responding to your ad. This data can be helpful as you look for other channels to promote your product on:

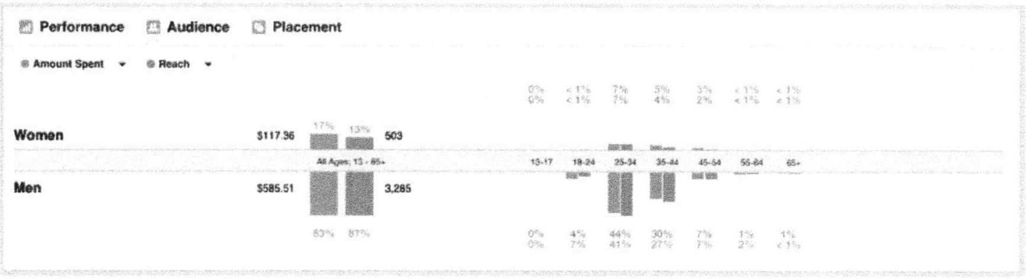

Facebook Ads' demographics

Final ask

Use the techniques above to keep your leads warm! Someone who's expressed interest in your product may need just a little nudge to order your product.

In the next chapter, we're going to talk about how to ask for the sale.

23

Close the deal: ask for the sale

"Software sales" feels sleazy, doesn't it?

We've all had bad experiences with salespeople.

> *"The salesman is the tiger, and the customer is the deer. The tiger has to eat, and you can't eat if you don't kill that deer. You have to go for the neck. Don't allow him to leave. But if you try to kill him too early, the deer will wake up and run away."*
> *- Manny Rosales, Car Salesman*[48]

You're different.

You're not selling someone else's wares; you're selling something *you built.* For you, doing the work to sell your product shouldn't feel sleazy.

You own the whole process: you've found a pain and built the solution. Now, you should have the confidence to say, "People need this; I need to tell them about it."

Good salesmanship is finding users and showing them how your app can help them. That's it. If that's what you're doing, you shouldn't feel sleazy.

This chapter covers tactics for *closing the deal.*[49]

---

[48] from episode 129 of the This American Life podcast

[49] I should note that if you have a low priced product that's in a marketplace (like the

Prioritize your leads

In the beginning, a simple spreadsheet is all you need to prioritize leads and make your first sales. Let's say you have a list of 100 people that are interested in your product. Put them in a spreadsheet that looks like this:

Prospects by Priority

Priority	First Name	Last Name	Email	$ Low	$ High	Ask Date	Follow Up Date	$ Converted
1	Mark	Tannen	mark.tannen@gmail.com	$19.00	$99.00	June 1, 2015	June 8, 2015	$99.00
2	Lucy	McGyver	lucy.mcgyver@gmail.com	$29.00	$199.00	June 15, 2015		$0.00
3	Julie	Junebug	julie.junebug@gmail.com	$9.00	$39.00			

Track your prospects in a spreadsheet

Your spreadsheet should have at least nine columns:

- **Priority:** How likely do you think this prospect is to convert to a paying customer?
- **First Name, Last Name, Email:** Keep track of who prospects are. If you're brave, you should track phone numbers too!
- **$ Low:** An estimate of the smallest amount they're likely to spend.
- **$ High:** An estimate of the most they would spend.
- **Ask Date:** What day did you ask for the sale?
- **Follow Up Date:** What day did you follow up?
- **$ Converted:** How much did they end up paying? If their answer is "no thank you," write down $0.

You objective is to force yourself to fill these all in. In the beginning, you're not going to like it. Pitching people to buy, and then following up, doesn't feel natural. Keep at it: when you start to see sales coming

---

iOS or Android app store), this chapter won't apply to you as much.

in, you might even enjoy it! Remember, you're providing people with something of value. It's worth helping them through the process of buying!

Ask for the money

There's a popular internet meme that originated on Futurama[50], where Bobby exclaims:

> *"Shut up and take my money!"*

People react with excitement when they see a product they want.

The flip-side for us as product *creators* is this:

> *"All right, I'm ready to take your money."*

At some point in our marketing process, we need to ask for the sale. For most of us, this will mean sending our prospects to a page with a price and a Buy Now button.

There are three places you'll likely have a call to action for people to buy:

- In an email
- In-product notification
- On your website

In an email

One of the last emails you'll send a prospect in a drip sequence, email course, or launch campaign is a "buy now" email. There are a few things you'll want to do in this email:

---

[50] Season 6, Episode 3

- **Have a clear call to action:** Make the link to the payment page prominent.
- **Create urgency:** A limited time offer can help nudge people to make a decision sooner.
- **Offer a discount:** Generally, 15% off is a good email offer (although this depends on your product).

Here's how Peel[51], a thin case for the iPhone, does their email:

Peel uses a limited time offer to get people to buy

In-product notification

If you have a software product, using in-app notifications is another way to get people to upgrade. This has become especially common with mobile apps, which have started to leverage in-app purchases on free apps.

[51] buypeel.com

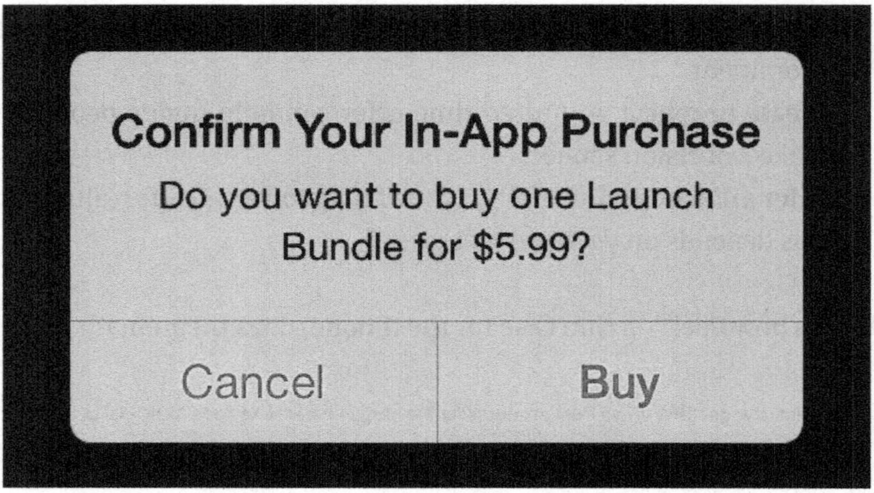

In-app purchases have a clear call to action

Marco Arment's podcasting app, Overcast, uses this model:[52]

> *Where does the money come from? Some features are locked or limited, and there's a single in-app purchase to unlock them all.*

His app is free to use, but advanced features (like cellular downloads and variable playback speeds) are only available in the paid version.

You can also use this approach in traditional desktop software, as well as web applications. Use push notifications, banners, and disabled states to urge users to upgrade.

---

[52] overcast.fm/skeptics_faq

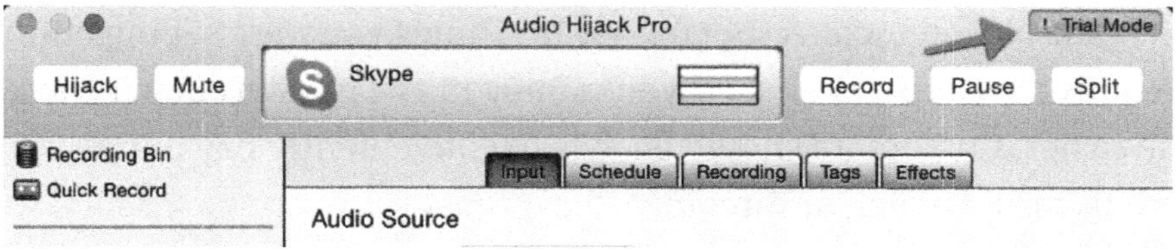

Audio Hijack Pro uses a small Trial Mode reminder

On your website

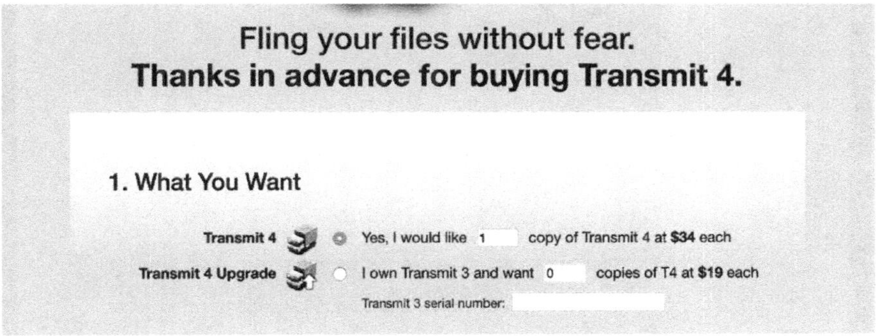

Panic.com has a well-designed "buy now" page

Make it easy

Be transparent with the user: tell them they're currently in a trial, or using a limited version of your software. Then, provide them with the benefits they'll get if they upgrade. Finally, give them a clear and easy way for them to give you money.

In the old days, collecting money for things you were selling online required customers to send you money in the mail. Today it *should* be easier. Customers should be able to conveniently pay online with credit card, PayPal, or Bitcoin.

Unfortunately, *paying* is often the worst part of the experience. Too many credit card forms look unprofessional. Many order forms require 3–4 different steps and 20–30 fields to complete! That's too many. Reduce as many steps as you can.

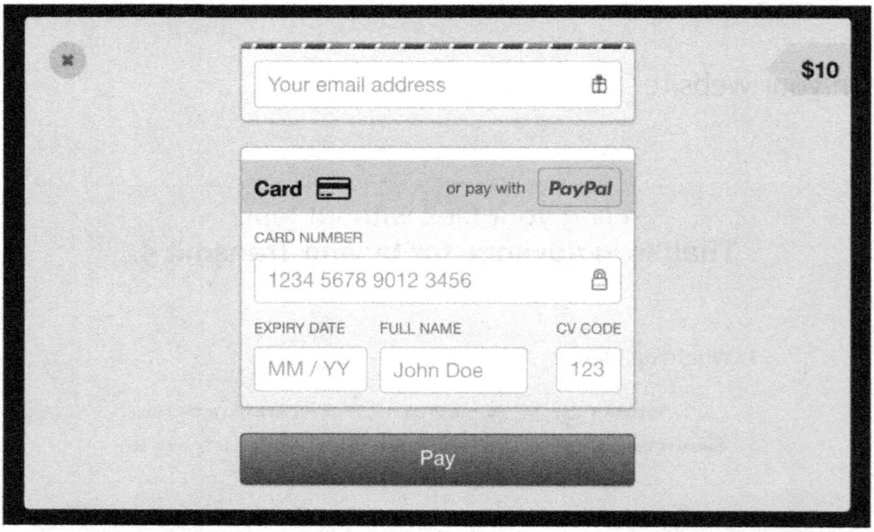

Gumroad's payment form is one step and only has five fields

I like how Gumroad's payment forms have one job: getting your credit card number. Everything else on the screen fades away. The form itself is well designed with large text, lots of padding in the form fields, and good defaults. No stock HTML form elements here!

Follow up

There's one secret to increasing conversions: follow up with your leads.

Most vendors don't do it, and it's the most successful way to secure a sale. This tactic can be done manually or as a part of an automatic flow. Master salesperson Steli Efti describes his approach:[53]

> *I have a simple philosophy - I follow up as many times as necessary until I get a response. I don't care what the response is as long as I get one. If someone tells me they need another 14 days to get back to me, I will put that in my calendar and ping them again in 14 days.*
>
> *If they tell me they are busy, and they don't have time right now, I will respond and ask them when they feel like a good time would be for me ping them. The key here is to actually keep following up. If someone tells me they are not interested - I leave them alone.*
>
> *But here is the kicker - if they don't respond at all, I will keep pinging them until they do.*

Following up like this makes many of us feel uncomfortable. However, it's worth doing; especially from the perspective of the customer.

Yesterday I received a phone call from the local ski resort. My family and I get a season's pass every year, and they were calling to remind us that the early bird deal would expire in 20 days. It turns out their email system hadn't been sending automated reminders. That phone call earned the ski resort another sale, and just as important, it kept me happy as a customer.

You've created an awesome solution. Be confident in asking people for their money!

---

[53] blog.close.io/follow-up

VI

Case Studies

24

Adam Wathan

- **Products:** Refactoring to Collections, Test-Driven Laravel, Kite-Tail.
- **Audience:** PHP programmers who use Laravel.

Adam Wathan has always been passionate about learning new things. In 2016, he discovered how he could earn an independent living doing it.

His book and video course, Refactoring to Collections, teaches PHP programmers how to apply functional programming principles to write clean, maintainable code.

My interview with Adam WathanWhat's your background? What's your work history?

I just went full-time on products. Previously, I was working as a software developer for a company called Tighten based in Chicago. They do client services consulting stuff; building web apps for clients. I worked with them for about a year and a half.

Before that, I was working with another agency that's local. I had one job in between there for another local consultancy that only lasted a couple of months. It turned out being a bad fit, and I was looking for something else really soon. But yeah, those are the only two real software development jobs I've ever had.

I've done a bunch of other random stuff too. I ran a recording studio in my house for a couple of years, recording bands for a living. That didn't work out (bands don't have money). [laughter] I also worked in the oil sands in northern Alberta for a couple of years.

Have you always been interested in programming?

As long as I can remember! As a kid I was obsessed with pro wrestling; it was my favorite thing in the world. When I was 9 – 10 years old, I found these text-based wrestling simulators you could download. You could make people wrestle each other and create wrestlers (this was the WWF Attitude era). I stumbled on a tutorial that taught you how to build a wrestling simulator in QBasic. I got it running on my parent's computer. It was fun just trying to make the computer do stuff.

What came after that?

In university, I was taking computer science, but I got burnt out and dropped out. There were other things I found way more fun, like music.

So I started this recording studio and started using this audio engineering software called Reaper (made by the same guy who built Winamp).

It turns out it's hackable. You could create plugins and write your features. It opened my eyes; I realized how much I love programming. I was having more fun improving the software than I was recording bands.

You have an excellent reputation online. People see you as an expert in the PHP community. How did you build that?

I am addicted to learning. When I get into something, I consume everything that exists in the world about that topic. I want to learn until I understand it as good as anyone. I used to play guitar like eight hours a day for like eight years. I got into like weightlifting and powerlifting to the point where I won a national powerlifting competition after two years. When I get into something, I just sink my teeth into, and I can't let it go.

What about building an audience? How did you get into that?

At first, I wasn't super intentional about it. Anytime I've gone into a new hobby I've always been active in online forums. I like participating in communities and talking to people.

Over time, I've developed a good reputation in almost any community that I've joined. For example, in the Reaper audio software world, you'll still see people starting threads on forums referencing a drum editing method I created.

It's the same with programming. For me, Twitter was the perfect place to get involved. To me, it seemed to be where all the programming discussions were happening. I just like participating in conversations, and share what I know.

When I was a kid, I would create walkthroughs for games like Doom. I love creating things for other people to consume.

What made you want to start blogging and podcasting?

It's just my natural way of being. I just want to be loud. I want to participate in a community and have strong opinions about things.

I don't blog super consistently, but it feels good to write stuff and put it out there. I like putting in a lot of effort, finishing something, and being able to share a complete thought. It might sound bad, but I'm addicted to putting something out there and having people see it.

Sharing stuff on Twitter has been just as rewarding. My friend Wes Bos has a huge Twitter following. And what seems to have contributed to his success is he's always sharing things; like a quick tip. I've been doing that more often. I'll get a hundred retweets on really simple lessons. It's been helpful for getting more followers and building a reputation.

I started my podcast because I had questions for Ryan Singer and I needed an excuse to get him to talk to me. I never started it as a platform to build an audience. It was an excuse to have some reason to get people to answer my questions. [laughter]

What made you decide to write a book?

I don't know if there was ever one moment where I decided: "Hey, I'm gonna be a product guy." But I've always loved creating things and sharing those creations with people. And the idea of making money from that sounded cool; being able to have freedom and control over what you're doing with your day.

My friend suggested that I create something tiny. He called it a "tripwire product:" something you can sell for really cheap (like $3 – $10). He gave me two main reasons to do it this way.

One reason is to get something done and get momentum in selling something online. You feel like: "Ok, I've sold something. I've taken someone's money for something I've made." That's a good step in the right direction to move on to something bigger.

The other reason is that it's useful for building your list. You now have real qualified people that are willing to spend money on things. Someone who has given you a dollar for something is much more likely to give you $200 for something else.

Why did you choose "refactoring to collections" as your topic?

I had been developing a reputation for the refactoring to collections stuff in PHP. I was trying to apply these functional programming ideas in PHP, got really excited about it and started sharing stuff on Twitter: "look I was able to take this code and do this with it. Isn't this cool?" People started coming to me with questions: "how would you do that with this piece of code?" I would try to figure out the answer and help people.

Eventually, I was thought: "hey, it would be kinda cool to put together a small 40 page PDF with some of my favorite tips and tricks for using this programming strategy."

After I had put together a simple landing page, I tweeted out:

> *"I'm writing a short book on refactoring with collections! Check it out if you're sick of ifs, loops, and variables."*

I went into it with this idea to build a 30 to 40 page PDF, but the next thing I knew it was like a hundred pages already. [laughter]

You ended up writing a pretty big book, and doing screencasts as well!

I remember having conversations with friends about how much to charge: \$9 – \$12? But by the time my book was finished, it was a 160-page book with four hours of accompanying screencasts. When I released it, my tiers were \$29, \$59, and \$135. All of which are dramatically higher than what I intended initially.

What was your launch sequence?

- Feb 23, 2016 – Announcement on Twitter.
- March 21, 2016 – Released sample chapter.
- March 29, 2016 – Released another sample chapter.
- April 7, 2016 – Wrote a blog post.
- April 10, 2016 – Sent my list a launch update.
- April 26, 2016 – Released another sample chapter.
- May 16, 2016 – Sent two-day launch notice to my list (shared a screenshot).
- May 18, 2016 – Launch day

Tell me more about the launch. How much revenue did you do?

The launch went a million times better than I could have ever hoped.

I had 14 sales on the night before the launch.

Then I sent the launch email at 7:15 am, and 81 sales came in.

I announced the launch on Twitter at 8:45 am, and by that time I'd made 133 sales.

At lunch, I was at 225 sales. The most surprising thing was that the expensive tier was outselling the low tier.

By the end of the day, I'd made 403 sales and had \$28,000 in revenue.

On the third day of the launch, I'd made 901 sales, and \$61,000 in income. It just kept going. I'm now well over \$100,000.

Wow. How did that feel?

I was losing my mind. That was the best day of my life. It's just such an amazing feeling to know you've created something that people are happy to pay money for. It's really awesome. I don't have any idea of what I'm doing. I'm just lucky to have a chance to teach an in-demand topic to the huge market of people that have enough money to spend on this sort of training.

Your story is awesome because it's obvious you hit a few things right. First, you had an enormous potential audience of PHP developers that wanted to level up. Like you mentioned: it's easy to get started using PHP, but eventually, a lot of those developers feel like they have holes in their knowledge. They're the kind of people that want to learn testing.

What can we learn from Adam's story?

When we look at Adam's success, three things stand out:

1. He is seen as an authority on testing. He built this reputation by being consistently helpful on Twitter, his blog, etc.
2. His reputation as a "helpful, smart person" lead to building an audience (both on Twitter and on his mailing list).
3. PHP developers are highly motivated to learn what he has to teach ("Shut up and take my money!")

Here's what this means for you

If you want to have success with a book, course, or membership site you need to:

- **Choose your market carefully.** Profitable products are born out sizeable markets (with money) who are highly motivated to improve their lives.
- **Build your reputation!** Get active in the community you want to serve. Be consistently helpful. Learn everything you can, and share what you're learning.
- **Grow your audience.** You need to have a way of building up a following. This way, when you launch, you'll have someone to launch to. I recommend a mailing list of at least 500 people before you think about building a paid product.

That first point is important. One thing that doesn't get talked about enough is that some target markets are better than others. Growth is a multiple of how big, reachable, spendthrifty your market is.

25

Tracy Osborn

Tracy Osborn is the author of Hello Web App

- **Products:** Hello Web App and WeddingLovely.
- **Audience:** non-programmers who want to build web apps.

After doing web and print design for years, Tracy caught the startup bug. In 2011, she taught herself Python and Django and created a wedding planner and vendor marketplace.

She realized that most online programming tutorials were intimidating; especially for beginners. Finally, in 2014 she did something about it. Tracy launched a Kickstarter for a new book, *Hello Web App*, that would meet novice programmers where they were at.

The Kickstarter was very successful: she exceeded her goal by 73%. To date, the book has earned over $25,000 in revenue.

Three things you can learn from Tracy:

1. **Build a network:** a big part of Tracy's success was her ability to create relationships in the Python community, and get people with big audiences to share her Kickstarter campaign.
2. **Importance of design:** the website for Hello Web App looks great. Tracy doesn't think you need to spend too much time on design, but making a few good decisions (like finding a good color scheme, and sticking to it) will pay dividends when people come to buy your product.
3. **Send cold emails:** Tracy sent individual emails to potential supporters. "I emailed pretty much everyone I knew who had influence in either the developer or designer spaces."

Tracy recently released her follow-up book, *Hello Web App - Intermediate Concepts*.

26

Nathan Kontny

Nate Kontny is the developer behind Draft

Product: Draft. He is also the new CEO of Highrise.

Audience: bloggers.

Nate had been blogging for years and was continually frustrated that there weren't tools like Git for collaborative editing. He decided to build his own. He shared it with his blogging friends, and they loved it.

Nate's audience is perfect for him: they hang out online in communities like Reddit. He'll spend a portion of his day answering writing, blogging, and marketing related questions on subreddits like blogging, startups, and design_critiques. You can tell that Nate genuinely enjoys writing, and being a part of the community he serves.

Do bloggers pay for things? In Nathan's case, yes: thousands of writers pay him $3.99 per month (or $39.99 per year). The surprising thing is this payment is *voluntary.* Draft is functional whether you pay for it or not. Despite this, Nate has been able to make a good living from his app.

Three things you can learn from Nate:

1. **Teaching is your best marketing:** Nate invests his time in Reddit threads, answering email, and on Twitter. He actively looks for opportunities to help people with their writing. And it works! When someone helps you for free, you're more likely to pay for their product.
2. **Practice, practice, practice:** just like going to the gym, Nate feels that good marketing is about practice. He forces himself to do writing exercises like: "Write ten headlines every day."
3. **Tell your story:** Nate makes himself relatable. He shares stories about his life, his marriage, and his family. This is a big part of his brand: he feels like someone you can trust.

27

Sean Fioritto

Product: Sketching With CSS.

Audience: web designers and developers.

After interacting with designers for years, Sean started to notice a trend: designers felt they couldn't express themselves creatively when they designed in the browser. Many wished they could go back to using Photoshop, even though it forced them to do everything twice (design *and* code). Sean decided to write *Sketching with CSS*, a book that helps designers learn how to design in the browser without having to give up any of their creative sensibilities.

Sean found it easy to connect with designers on sites like Designer News. Web designers are on their computers all day and are extremely social. Their community is also tight knit: they visit many of the same sites, go to design oriented conferences, and listen to the similar podcasts.

The other benefit of this audience is that they're used to paying for tools (computers, software, books). In Sean's first month, he made $5,020 in pre-orders. The following month, when he launched, he earned another $5,000.

Three things you can learn from Sean:

1. **Be the target customer.** Sean isn't a designer and found it difficult to be a part of their world consistently. In retrospect, he wishes he'd chosen "software developers" as his audience.
2. **Don't start with an idea.** Sean tried and failed multiple times to build a product that attracted customers. Finally, he decided to start with an audience, discover their needs, and develop a product to solve their problems. It worked! "Starting with an idea is a self-centered way to build a product."

3. **Use your time wisely.** If you're bootstrapping your product, you can't waste time. Be as efficient as you can. Get off Twitter and Slack!

28

Garrett Dimon

Garrett Dimon built Sifter on the side

Product: Sifter (acquired). Garrett is now runs marketing at Wildbit.
Audience: web developers, project managers, founders.

Garrett was frustrated that his clients wouldn't use the bug trackers on the market. He set out to make something better: a tracker his customers would use. Initially, he decided to make it open source. However, after sharing it with other developers, their advice was to turn it into to a SaaS app instead. The result was Sifter, a web application he's been running profitable since day one.

Building an audience was almost accidental for Garrett. He hadn't set out to build a business, so he shared his journey. People resonated with his openness and curiosity.

Your audience doesn't need to be huge, but your launch will be a lot easier if you have one. Garrett had a pre-launch list with 1,000 email addresses, 2,000 Twitter followers, and nearly 6,000 people subscribed to his RSS feed. That audience helped him generate $1,000 in revenue in his first month of business.

Businesses (especially software development companies) pay money for tools. Garrett promises them Sifter will simplify their bug tracking, which in turn saves them time and money.

Three things you can learn from Garrett:

1. **Ask yourself, "Do you want to start a business?"** Garrett warns developers that there is a lot more to running an app business than writing code. "If you just want to create stuff, and write code, starting a business is not the best way to do that," he says.
2. **Don't compete on features.** It's possible to do *less* than the competition and do better. Deliver outcomes for your users as opposed to new features, and they'll be much happier.

3. **Frustration with existing products isn't enough.** Don't build a business just because you don't like the current offerings. You have to be genuinely passionate about the problem. "Once you start building, you quickly learn that all of the shortcomings in the products that they hate weren't born out of laziness, but simple tradeoffs." Garrett has always been genuinely passionate about workflows, which makes Sifter a good fit for him.

Garrett's written a book about the lessons he learned building Sifter called Starting and Sustaining.

Closing thoughts

I've been thinking a lot about makers; the people who put themselves on the line to create products that people use.

Most people don't create, they consume. **You're different.** You've sat at your computer day after day writing code, looking towards the day where you'd ship your product. Putting something out into the world takes guts. You've done it.

Secretly, we're all scared that our project will fail. We've poured our heart and soul into creating it, and we hope that people will receive it with open arms.

If your first attempt at marketing a product doesn't work, don't despair. **Keep making things.** Most of us have to try multiple times before we find something that works.

> *Stuart Butterfield was working on a game called Glitch. He and his team had invested two years of development time in the project. They were hoping for a massive launch that would drive thousands of gamers to sign up in multiplayer mode. The launch failed: they just couldn't attract enough players.*
>
> *Stuart and his team decided to pivot and launched a little internal chat app they'd been using. They called it Slack. If you've paid attention to tech news, you know that Slack has experienced incredible traction. At the time of writing, Slack is valued at $2.8 billion dollars and has over 750,000 daily users.*[54]

[54] techcrunch.com/2015/04/16/used-daily-by-750k-workers-slack-raises-160m-to-value-collaboration-startup-at-2-8b/

Sometimes you just need another turn at bat. Keep at it. Keep shipping! Learn from the response you receive. Focus on getting better.

> *"I'm convinced...half of what separates the successful entrepreneurs from the non-successful ones is pure perseverance."*
> *– Steve Jobs*

At the beginning of this book, I told you about my goal: that more developers would earn an income from the things they create. Supporting independent makers is a purpose I'd like to pursue for the rest of my life.

I'm cheering for you! I'd love to hear about what you're making. You can reach me at words@megamaker.co.

Finally, I want to thank you. When you purchase a self-published work like this, you're supporting something bigger: a movement of independent makers who can make a living from the things they create. Thank you, thank you, thank you.

Let's connect soon,

Justin Jackson

@mijustin

Made in the USA
Monee, IL
04 November 2026

67378298R00134